C&T Asian Language Series

实用汉语课本

Practical Chinese Reader I
Patterns and Exercises

Revised and Expanded
Simplified Character Edition

汉字作业簿

简体字本

【语法结构】
【翻译】【词序】【用词】【问答】【作文】

陈曼丽
Madeline Men-li Chu

Cheng & Tsui Company

About the Author

Madeline Men-li Chu is Associate Professor of Chinese language and literature at Kalamazoo College. Prior to her appointment to the endowed chair at Kalamazoo College in 1988, she taught at Oberlin College (Assistant Professor and then Asia House Director, 1978-80), Connecticut College (Assistant Professor, 1980-86), and the University of Massachusetts, Amherst (Five Colleges Associate Professor, 1986-88). While still in Taiwan, she taught at the prestigious First Girls' High School and the World College of Journalism. She has taught beginning to advanced language courses, both modern and classical, as well as literature in translation and original language literature. She has authored many articles and contributed to major works, such as the *Indian Companion to Classical Chinese Literature* and *Waiting for the Unicorn*. Madeline Chu received her B.A. degree in Chinese language and literature from National Taiwan University, and her M.A. and Ph.D degrees from the University of Arizona, Tuscon.

Cheng & Tsui Company
25 West Street
Boston, MA 02111-1268 USA
e-mail ct@world.std.com

Library of Congress Catalog Number: 89-051123

New and Expanded Simplified Character Edition ISBN 0-88727-233-9
New and Expanded Simplified Character Edition ISBN 0-88727-175-8

Printed in the United States of America

Companion textbook, writing workbooks, computer software, video tapes and audio tapes are available from the publisher.

PUBLISHER'S NOTE

The Cheng & Tsui Company is pleased to announce the most recent volume of the *C&T Asian Language Series,* the new and expanded edition of *Practical Chinese Reader I: Patterns and Exercises.* This workbook supplements the highly successful introductory Chinese language textbook *Practical Chinese Reader I,* developed by the Beijing Language Institute.

The C&T Asian Language Series is designed to publish and widely distribute quality language texts as they are completed by teachers at leading educational institutions. *The C&T Asian Language Series* is devoted to significant works in the field of Asian languages developed in the United States and elsewhere.

We welcome readers' comments and suggestions concerning the publications in this series. Please contact the following members of the Editorial Board:

Professor Shou-hsin Teng, Chief Editor
Dept. of Asian Languages and Literature
University of Massachusetts, Amherst, MA 01003

Professor Samuel Cheung
Dept. of East Asian Languages, University of California, Berkeley, CA 94720

Professor Ying-che Li
Dept. of East Asian Languages, University of Hawaii, Honolulu, HI 96822

Professor Timothy Light
Dept. of Religion, Western Michigan University, Kalamazoo, MI 49008

Professor Ronald Walton
Dept. of Hebrew and East Asian Languages and Literature
University of Maryland, College Park, MD 20742

CONTENTS

ACKNOWLEDGEMENTS

First, I would like to thank those who used the 1989, 1990, 1992 and 1993 editions of the *Practical Chinese Reader I: Patterns and Exercises.* Your interest and encouragement are greatly appreciated. This volume brings the simplified character version up to date with the various expansions and revisions of this book that have taken place in the past few years. It includes more notes for clarification and more communicative exercises than the earlier issue. It also uses a different, and clearer, typesetting of the Chinese characters.

Many people have provided valuable assistance in the writing and revision of this book during its earlier stages. The beginning of the first draft was made possible by a Mellon Grant awarded by the Executive Committee of the Five Colleges Foreign Language Resource Center, Amherst, Massachusetts. I want to thank my former colleagues at the Five Colleges: Ted Yao, Grace Fong, Alvin Cohen and Ling-hsia Yeh who used the first and second drafts of the exercises in their classes and offered me valuable comments. My special thanks go to Shou-hsin Teng of the University of Massachusetts: it was under his leadership that the PCR-supplementary materials project was initiated. The support and suggestions of members of the editorial boards Cheng & Tsui Publishing Company were most useful in guiding me in the revision of the first edition.

Kalamazoo College provided me with the necessary facilities and personnel assistants, which made the subsequent revisions at each stage much easier. I want to thank Katheryn Rajnak, Professor of Physics, and Fusen Han, editor and manager of the Xia Li Baren Software for Macintosh, for their help in making the computer more friendly. For the most recent revisions, my thanks go to Jane Parish Yang, Ned VanderVen and Huang Xuefeng for their valuable comments, to Sun Qingshun and Chen Ruofan for their help with the typing and to my students at Kalamazoo College for their continuing feedback. Of course, I am solely responsible for any remaining errors and shortcomings.

Spiritual support has always been the most important energizing force behind my work. As always, my husband, John, and my sons, Robert and Andy, have supported me in every way. They make me feel that my work is important. My family, therefore, deserves the ultimate credit for this book.

– Madeline Chu
Kalamazoo College
Summer 1995

INTRODUCTION

Practical Chinese Reader I: Patterns and Exercises is a book of sentence patterns and written exercises, published as a companion volume for the textbook *Practical Chinese Reader I. The Practical Chinese Reader* series has a particular strength in introducing practical expressions and helping initiate useful conversations. However, one shortcoming of the texts is their failure to systematically introduce the basic grammatical structure of Chinese, an essential component in developing a useful understanding of the language and in establishing a solid foundation for more advanced use of the language. Supplementary materials are necessary to make these texts effective.

Practical Chinese Reader I: Patterns and Exercises was written to meet this need. With pattern illustrations and exercises, it provides supplementary materials to assure effective use of the language elements introduced in the textbook. For a language such as Chinese that has no inflectional endings but depends heavily on syntax to express grammatical relations, pattern analysis is of ultimate importance. The pattern illustrations provide a starting point for the accompanying exercises. The incorporated exercises would help students establish a systematic understanding of the linguistic and cultural elements introduced in the textbook and to increase their sensitivity of the general characteristics of the Chinese language.

Five types of exercises are included: (1) *Translation*, to familiarize the student with the sentence patterns associated with each lesson and offer enough opportunity for hands-on exercises by applying the patterns for making meaningful statements; (2) *Word Order*, to train the student to observe the important sequence of elements in each type of sentence and explore different possibilities of ordering these elements; (3) *Choice of Words*, to sharpen the student's sensitivity to the semantic and grammatical nuances of words and phrases, and the roles they play in different statements; (4) *Answering Questions*, to help the student review the content as well as the grammatical points of the lessons in the textbook and to enhance their ability to communicate in the language; and (5) *Composition*, to train the students to organize their thoughts around the acquired Chinese vocabularies and sentence patterns and to connect sentences into paragraphs, so as to express themselves in Chinese actively and meaningfully.

Together, these exercises provide plenty of opportunities for the students to learn to use the language in a wide range of realistic situations. They are designed to help the student in the reading and writing aspects of leaning process. They encourage the student to practice writing characters with a purpose and they provide sufficient opportunity to enable him/her to become familiar with these characters. At the same time, they offer variety and eliminate the monotony caused by the conventional assignment of writing the same character time and again. They reinforce the student's understanding of the language through doing the exercises. Furthermore, because these exercises are organized according to the level of difficulty, they may be straightforward, yet interesting, challenging, yet not frustrating. Three vocabulary finding lists, as well as two character finding lists, are included as appendices; this will allow the student to easily locate characters or vocabulary items. Additionally, a simplified-regular character conversion table is attached for easy reference.

It is the author's hope that the pattern illustrations, language-use explanations, examples and exercises will reduce to a minimum the need for in-class factual exposition so that class time may be more efficiently used in the development of listening and speaking skills.

ABBREVIATIONS

Adj	....	Adjective
Adv	....	Adverb
Co-V	....	Co-verb
Conj	....	Conjunction
Exp	....	Expression
IM	....	Initiation Marker
Inf	....	Information
MM	....	Manner Marker
Modif	....	Modifier
Neg	....	Negative
NP	....	Noun Phrase
Obj	....	Object
Pred	....	Predicate
Pron	....	Pronoun
Q-w	....	Question Word
Subj	....	Subject
V	....	Verb
V-act	....	Verb of Action
V-ex	....	Verb of Existence
V-id	....	Verb of Identity
V-mtn	....	Verb of Motion
V-st	....	Verb of State
VP	....	Verb Phrase

Exercise I
(Lessons 1-3)

A. 翻译 Translation: Apply the illustrated pattern to translate the sentences into Chinese.

Pattern #1: **Descriptive Sentence**: Describing the state of people (or things).

	The subject		**is in this state.**
	Subj: NP	<Neg.>	Predicate: V-state
[Examples]:	我	不	忙.
	他们		都很好.

1. He is not busy.

   Tā bù máng ✓

2. They are fine.

   Tāmen hǎo ✓

3. Both my older brother and my younger brother are very busy.

   dì dwǒ gēge wǒ dìdi dōu hěn máng ✓

4. His younger brother is also very busy.

   Tā dìdi yě hěn máng ✓

5. His older brother and my older brother are both nice.

   Tā gēge wǒ gēge dōu hǎo ✓

6. Gubo is fine.

   Gubo hǎo ✓

7. Palanka is busy, too.

   Palanka yě máng ✓

8. You are not busy. They are not busy, either.

   nimen bù máng, Tāmen yě bù máng ✓

9. They are both quite well.

   Tāmen dōu hěn hǎo ✓

10. All of us are also not very busy.

   dǒmen yě dōu hěn máng ✓

   A⁺

1

Exercise I (Cont.)

B. 翻译 Translation : Apply the illustrated patterns to translate the sentences into Chinese.

Pattern #2:   **Interrogative Sentence**: Using Question-word 吗 to verify a statement.

	The subject is in this state	right?
	Statement: sentence	Q-w 吗
[Example]:	他 不 忙	吗?

Pattern #3:   **Interrogative Sentence**: Using Question-word 呢 to compare situations.

	Subj. 1	is in this state.	Subj. 2	the same?
	Subj. 1	Pred. 1	Subj. 2	Q-w 呢?
[Example]:	我	好,	你	呢?

1. "How are you?" "I'm very well, and you?"

2. How is your older brother?

3. Is neither his older brother nor his younger brother nice?

4. Are you busy?

5. Are they also busy?

6. I am not very busy. How about you?

7. I am fine. How about you?

8. His older brother is busy. How about his younger brother?

9. You are not very busy. How about him?

10. Both my older brother and younger brother are not very busy. How about your brothers?

2

Christine Fahens   10/1/99

Exercise I (Cont.)

C. 词序 Word Order: Rearrange the elements of each entry to make a grammatical sentence.

Note: Refer to the patterns listed previously and the following order of modifiers.

Subject			**Predicate**
[Subj.]	（也）		<Neg.> 都 <Neg.> 很 忙 吗?

1. 都   他们   忙   很   ✓
    2   1   4   3

2. 好   很   也   他   ✓
    4   3   2   1

3. 我   忙   呢   不   你   ✓
    1   3   5   2   4

4. 都   他哥哥   不忙   他弟弟   ✓
    3   1   4   2

5. 不   也   你   吗   忙   ✓
    3   2   1   5   4

6. 吗   好   你   ✓
    3   2   1

7. 忙   很   吗   都   他们   ✓
    4   3   5   2   1

8. 也   忙   他哥哥   很   ✓
    2   4   1   3

9. 呢   你   他们   都   好   很   ✓
    6   5   1   2   4   3

10. 都   他们   很   不   忙   也   ✓
    2   1   5   4   6   3
    3   2

A

3

Exercise I (Cont.)

D. 用词 Choice of Words: Choose the most appropriate word or phrase from the list to complete a grammatical sentence.

1. 我很好, 你 _____ ?
     (a) 吗   (b) 呢   (c) 也

2. 我不忙, 他们 _____ 不忙.
     (a) 都   (b) 很   (c) 也

3. 他们 _____ 不忙吗?
     (a) 也都   (b) 都很   (c) 也很

4. 你忙 _____ ?
     (a) 吗   (b) 呢   (c) 也

5. 他 _____ 忙.
     (a) 很不   (b) 不也   (c) 不很

6. 他们也都 _____ 好.
     (a) 忙   (b) 很   (c) 吗

7. 你哥哥, 我哥哥 _____ 不忙.
     (a) 都   (b) 很   (c) 也

8. _____ 都忙吗?
     (a) 你   (b) 他们   (c) 他不

9. 我很忙, 你 _____ 忙吗?
     (a) 也很   (b) 也不   (c) 很

10. 他哥哥很好, 他弟弟 _____ ?
     (a) 吗   (b) 呢   (c) 也

Exercise I (Cont.)

E. 问答 Questions: Answer the following questions.

Note: Assume that in numbers 1-5 the two subjects concerned are in the same situation and that in numbers 6-10 they are not.

1. 我不忙,你呢?

2. 他们都很好, 你呢?

3. 我好, 你呢?

4. 我很好,你好吗?

5. 他很忙, 你呢?

6. 我弟弟很好,你弟弟呢?

7. 我不忙,你忙吗?

8. 我哥哥,(我)弟弟都很好. 你哥哥,(你)弟弟也都很好吗?

9. 他不好. 他哥哥好吗?

10. 你哥哥很忙. 你弟弟不忙吗?

Exercise II
(Lessons 4-6)

A. 翻译 Translation: Apply the illustrated pattern to translate the sentences into Chinese.

<u>**Pattern #4**</u>:   **Ascriptive Sentence**: Using verb-of-identification 是 to identify the subject by profession / nationality / relation to others, etc.

	This subject		**is**	**of this identity**.
	Person(s)/Thing(s)	\<neg.\>	V-id 是	ID of person(s)/thing(s)
[Examples]:	他们		是	大夫.
	这	不	是	王(Wang) 大夫.

1. He is Palanka's father.

   Ta shi palanka de baba. ✓

2. They are not Chinese.

   Tamen bu shi zhongguo ren! ✓

3. That is my mother's friend.

   nà shì wo māma de pengyou ✓

4. My older brother's friend is a doctor.

   wo gege de pengyou shi daifu ✓

5. Are you a teacher?

   zhù shi laoshi ma? ✓

6. Isn't any of them his friend?

   Tamen dou bu shi Ta depengyou ✓ma?

7. This is not my younger brother's book.

   zhe bui shi wo didi de shū ✓

8. This is his car. That is also his car.

   zhe shi tade chē. Na ye shi ta de chē ✓

9. Our doctor is also our friend.

   wǒmen
   Wǒmen de daifu yě shi dou de pengyou ✓

10. Not all Chinese language teachers are Chinese.

   hanyou bu dou shi zhongguo ren ✓

Exercise II (Cont.)

B. 翻译 **Translation:** Apply the illustrated pattern to translate the sentences into Chinese.

Pattern #5:   **Interrogative Sentences:** Using question-words 谁, 谁的 or 哪国人 to inquire identity of person(s) / thing(s).

	(a) This/These person(s)	**is/are**	**of what id/nationality?**
	NP - person(s)	是	Q-word 谁 / 哪国人
[Example]	她	是	哪国人?
	(b) The person(s)/thing(s)	**is/are**	**whose relation / belonging?**
	NP - person(s)/thing(s)	是	Q-word 谁的 + NP
[Example]	这	是	谁的汉语书?
	(c) Which person(s)	**is/are**	**one(s) with this identity?**
	Q-word 谁	是	NP - person
[Example]	谁	是	大夫?
	(d) Whose relation/belonging	**is/are**	**one(s) with this identity?**
	Q-word 谁的 + NP	是	NP-person(s)/thing(s)
[Example]	谁的车	是	美(Mei3)国车?

Note: In a Chinese sentence, an indicative noun or pronoun such as 这, 那, 他/她(们) and 他/她(们)的, generally appears before the verb-id 是.

1. Who is she?

Tā shì shéi? ✔

2. Who is a doctor?

shéi shì dàifu?

3. Which one is your Chinese language teacher?

Shéi shì nǐ Hànyǔ lǎoshi? ✔

4. Who is her older brother?

shéi shì tā gēge? ✔

5. Whose car is this?

Zhè shì shei de chē? ✔

6. Whose car is a Japanese* car? [*=item included in the supplementary vocabulary list.]

Shéi de chē shì rìběn chē? ✔

7. What is the nationality of your Chinese language teacher?

nǐ de Hànyu lǎoshi shì nǎ guó rén ✔

8. Who are your teacher's friends?

Shéi shì nǐ lǎoshi de péngyou ✔

9. Which (of them) are Chinese and which are American*? [*=supplementary vocabulary item]

nǎ ... shì zhōngguó de nǎ shì měiguo de? ✔

10. What kind of car [use "made in which country"] is her car?

Tā de chē shì nǎ guó chē? ✔   **A**

Exercise II (Cont.)

C. 词序 Word Order: Rearrange the elements of each entry to make a grammatical sentence.

1. 书   是   那

2. 爸爸   是   我   这

3. 车   的   我   这   是

4. 吗   是   哥哥   这   她

5. 大夫   不   是   车   的   那

6. 你们   她   是   朋友   的   吗

7. 是   书   弟弟   的   那   也

8. 不   我   大夫   是

9. 谁的   老师   汉语   是   中(Zhong1)国人

10. 大夫   哪国   是   人   你的

Exercise II (Cont.)

D. 用词 Choice of Words: Choose the most appropriate word or phrase from the list to complete a grammatical sentence.

1. 这 ____c____ 我妈妈.
   (a) 也   (b) 不   (c) 是

2. 他们 ____b____ 我朋友.
   (a) 好   (b) 是   (c) 不

3. 这是你 ____b____ 书吗?
   (a) 爸爸   (b) 的   (c) 中 (Zhong1) 国

4. 我爸爸,我妈妈 ____c____ 大夫.
   (a) 都   (b) 好   (c) 都是

5. 她弟弟 ____b____ 我朋友.
   (a) 这是   (b) 也是   (c) 是也

6. 这 ____a____ 我妈妈的车.
   (a) 不是   (b) 都   (c) 也

7. 我 ____c____ 车很好.
   (a) 不   (b) 是   (c) 的

8. 这是谁 ____b____ 书?
   (a) 呢   (b) 的   (c) 吗

9. 这不是你的车,是 ____b____ 车?
   (a) 哪国   (b) 谁的   (c) 吗

10. 你的朋友是 ____a____ 人?
    (a) 哪国   (b) 谁   (c) 谁的

Exercise II (Cont.)

E. 问答 Questions: Answer the following questions according to your real-life situation.

1. 谁是你的汉语老师？

2. 你的老师是哪国人？

3. 你妈妈是老师吗？

4. 你哥哥是大夫吗？

5. 谁是老师？ 谁是大夫？

6. 谁是法(Fa3 or Fa4) 国人？

7. 你老师的车是美(Mei3) 国车吗？

8. 你爸爸的车是哪国车？

9. 谁的车是德(De2) 国车？

10. 你的大夫是谁？

Exercise III
(Review: Lessons 1-6)

A. 翻译 **Translation**: Apply the patterns learned so far to translate the following sentences into Chinese.

1. Are all doctors very nice? Are they all very busy?

2. Not all doctors are very nice. Not all of them are very busy, either.

3. His mother is a doctor. She is very busy. His father is also a doctor. He is not very busy.

4. Neither my mother nor my father is a doctor. They are teachers.

5. Her mother and her father are both very busy. They are both well, too.

6. This is my younger brother. That is my younger brother's friend.

7. My younger brother is a doctor. His friend is also a doctor.

8. That is his car. His car is an American car.

9. His American car is very good.

10. My car is a Chinese car. It [use "my car"] is also very good.

Exercise III (Cont.)

B. 作文 Composition: Write a short passage describing the following picture. For example, you may refer to the two vehicles in terms of their relative position from where you stand, you may write about the size, the quality, the ownership, and their country of origin.

·1973 VW BUG·

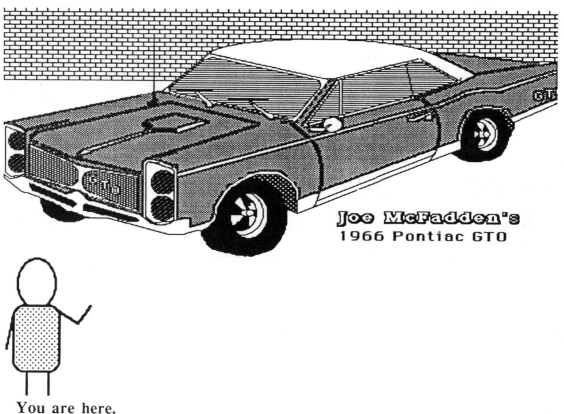

Joe McFadden's
1966 Pontiac GTO

You are here.

Exercise III (Cont.)

C. 作文 **Composition**: write a short passage describing the following picture. For example, you may refer to the two books in terms of their relative position from where you stand, you may write about the size, the content, the quality, and the ownership of them.

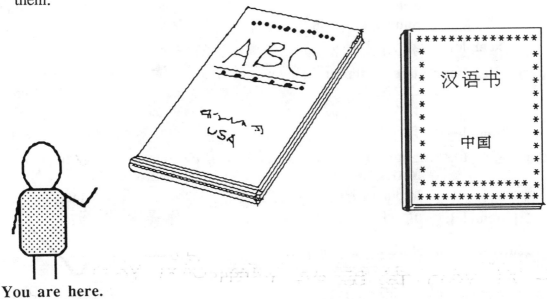

You are here.

D. 作文 **Composition:** Write a short paragraph about one of your friends' family. For example you may write about his/her parents, brothers, doctors, friends. You may also add a few things about some of these people in terms of their nationalities, professions, and belongings.

(handwritten top margin: dōu, yě, bù + v + adv + adj)

Exercise IV
(Lessons 7-9)

A. 翻译 **Translation**: Apply the illustrated pattern to translate the sentences into Chinese.

Pattern #6: **Narrative Sentence:** Using Verb-of-action to describe habit or action.

Someone		**does**	**something**.
Subj: NP-person	\<neg.>	V-act	Obj.: NP

[Example]: 我朋友   不   喝   茶.

Pattern #7: **Imperative Sentence:** Using word of request 请 to make a polite request.

Please	**do**	**this**.
请	V-act	Obj.: NP

[Example]: 请   看   地图.

Pattern #8: **Interrogative Sentence:** using idiom 请问 to make a polite inquiry.

May I ask	**this question**?
Idiom 请问	interrogative sentence

[Example]: 请问   你是大夫吗?

1. He smokes. None of his friends smoke.

Tā xī yān. tā de péngyou dōu bù xī yān. ✓

2. All my friends read Chinese newspapers* [*=supplementary vocabulary item].

wǒ (dōu) de péngyou kàn Hànyǔ bào. ✗

3. Our Chinese language teacher doesn't drink milk*.

wǒmen de Hànyǔ lǎoshī bù hē niúnǎi.

4. I'm reading a Chinese language textbook.

wǒ kàn Hànyǔ shū. ✓

5. Both my older brother and my younger brother study Chinese language.

wǒ gēge wǒ dìdi dōu xué Hànyǔ. ✓

6. Please look at the map of China. [Use the character for "Zhong1" if you can.]

qǐng kàn zhōngguó dìtú ✓

7. May I ask, who drinks tea?

qǐngwèn shéi hē chá

8. May I ask, is this your map?

qǐngwèn zhè shì nǐ de dìtú ma? ✗

9. Could you tell me who is Mr. Ding? [The character for Ding is 丁.]

Qǐng nǐ gàosù wǒ shéi Dīng?

10. Could you tell me what you are watching?

Qǐng nǐ gàosù wǒ nǐ kàn shénme? ✓

Exercise IV (Cont.)

B. 翻译 Translation: Apply the illustrated pattern to translate the sentences into Chinese.

Pattern #9:   **Interrogative Sentence**: Using Question-word 什么 / 什么+ to inquire about thing(s), or kind of thing(s) or person(s).

	(a) **This**	**is**	**what <+>**?
	NP-indicative pron	V-id	Q-word 什么 / 什么 + NP
[Example]:	这	是	什么 / 什么车?
	(b) **What <+>**		**is / are in this state**?
	Q-word 什么 / 什么 + NP		V-state
[Example]:	什么 / 什么车		好?

1. What's that? [Literally: "That is what?"   (See **Note** on p. 7.)]

2. What kind of map is that? [Literally: "That is what map?"]

3. What kind of pen/pencil* is this [*=supplementary vocabulary item]?

4. What kind of car does your friend have? [Literally: "Your friend's car is what car?"]

5. May I ask, what would you like to drink? [= ...what do you drink?]

6. Could you tell me [= May I ask] what books are good?

7. May I ask, what are you studying?

8. Who is that? [Use "What person...."]

9. Could you tell me what is "pi2jiu3"*?

10. Who is greeting [= welcoming] her?

Exercise IV (Cont.)

C. 翻译 Translation: Apply the illustrated pattern to translate the sentences into Chinese.

Pattern #10: **Ascriptive Sentence**: Using Verb-of-identification 姓 or 叫 to identity the subject by name.

The subject		**is named**	**so-and-so**.
NP-person	<neg.>	V-id 姓	NP-family name
NP-person	<neg.>	V-id 叫	NP-given/full name
NP-thing	<neg.>	V-id 叫	NP-name

[Examples]:　我的老师　　　　　姓　　　王 (Wang2).

　　　　　　　他　　　不　　　叫　　　王大好.

Note: Family name precedes one's title of addressing; for example: 谢大夫.

1. May I ask, whose family name is Wang?

2. Our doctor's family name is Wang and his given name is Zhong1shu1.

3. My friend's younger brother is named Ding1 Da4zhong1.

4. He is an American*. His last name is Johnson and his first name is Don.

5. My friend's Chinese car is nicknamed "Shanghai* Doctor." [*supplementary vocabulary item]

6. Is your Chinese friend's family name Che? [Do you know the character for che1?]

7. Dr. Ding's older brother's name is Da4you3.

8. Mr. Che, the teacher [=Che1 Lao3shi1] is very busy.

9. Mrs.* Xie4's mother's maiden name is Huang2 (黄) and her full name is Huang2 Da4mei3 (美).

10. Both Dr. Xie and Dr. Che have the given name Mei3fu1.

Exercise IV (Cont.)

D. 词序 Word Order: Rearrange the elements of each entry to make a grammatical sentence.

1. 都   我们   烟   不   吸

2. 什么   是   那

3. 这   地图   是   的   谁

4. 茶   请   喝

5. 她   丁云(Ding Yun)   丁(Ding)   姓   叫

6. 您   姓   贵   请   问

7. 哪国   是   她   留学生

8. 什么   地图   你   看

9. 也   老师   你们   的   车   姓   吗

10. 叫   朋友   的   他   大生   不

Exercise IV (Cont.)

E. 用词 Choice of Words: Choose the most appropriate word or phrase from the list to complete a grammatical sentence.

1. 这是 ___C___ 地图？
   (a) 哪   (b) 谁   (c) 什么

2. ___b___ 是大夫？
   (a) 哪   (b) 谁   (c) 什么

3. 他是 ___C___ 人？
   (a) 哪   (b) 谁   (c) 什么

4. 那是 ___b___ 的书？
   (a) 我   (b) 谁   (c) 什么

5. 这不是你的车，是 ___b___ 车？
   (a) 哪国   (b) 谁的   (c) 什么

6. ___b___ 汉语老师 不是中(Zhong1)国人？
   (a) 哪国   (b) 谁的   (c) 什么

7. 美(Mei3)国笔(bi3)不好，___C___ 笔好？
   (a) 哪国   (b) 谁的   (c) 什么

8. 这不是汉语书，是 ___C___ 书？
   (a) 哪国   (b) 谁的   (c) 什么

9. 那不是中国地图，是 ___a___ 地图？
   (a) 哪国   (b) 谁的   (c) 什么

10. 你哥哥的好朋友是 ___b___ ？
    (a) 哪   (b) 谁   (c) 什么

Exercise IV (Cont.)

F. 用词 Choice of Words: Choose the most appropriate word or phrase from the list to complete a grammatical sentence.

1. _____, 你们都吸烟吗？
    (a) 请   (b) 请问   (c) 请你

2 他不 _____ 茶.
    (a) 是   (b) 好   (c) 喝

3. "那是 _____ 车?" "那是日本(Ri4ben3)* 车." [*=supplementary word]
    (a) 谁的   (b) 哪国   (c) 什么

4. 古波(Gubo) _____ 朋友叫帕兰卡(Palanka).
    (a) 是   (b) 好   (c) 的

5. 她的弟弟 _____ 谢汉夫.
    (a) 姓   (b) 叫   (c) 是不

6. 我们都 _____ 汉语.
    (a)学习   (b) 是   (c) 好

7. 请问, 您 _____ 姓?
    (a) 什么   (b) 贵   (c) 谢

8. 你们的大夫不 _____ 谢吗？
    (a) 是   (b) 叫   (c) 姓

9. _____ 不学习汉语,他妈妈学习汉语.
    (a) 老师谢   (b) 谢大夫   (c) 大夫谢

10. "你看 _____ 书?" "我看汉语书."
    (a) 哪国   (b) 什么   (c) 谁的

Exercise IV (Cont.)

G. 问答 **Questions:**

<u>Note</u>: Answer questions 1-4 according to the picture of Exercise III-B.

1. 这是什么？

2. 这是谁的车？

3. 这是哪国车？

4. 那也是美(Mei3)国车吗？

5. 你喝茶吗？你汉语老师呢？

6. 请问，谁吸烟？

7. 你爸爸妈妈都吸烟吗？

8. 丁云(Ding Yun)是什么学院的学生？

Exercise V
(Lessons 10-12)

A. 翻译 Translation: Apply the illustrated pattern to translate the sentences into Chinese.

Pattern # 11: **Ascriptive Sentence:** Using Verb-of-existence 在 / 住 / 住在 to indicate location of the subject.

The subject		**lives at / is at**	**this place.**
NP	\<neg.\>	V-ex 在 / 住 / 住在	NP - place
[Example]: 谢老师	不	住在	宿舍.

Pattern #12: **Interrogative Sentence:** Using Q-word 吗 or 哪儿 to inquire about location of the subject.

(a) **Someone/something** **is at this place** **right?**

	Sentence of Location		Q-word 吗
[Example]:	丁云 (Ding Yun)	在宿舍	吗?

(b) **Subject** **lives at / is at** **where?**

	NP - person/thing	V-exist 在 / 住 / 住在	Q-word 哪儿
[Example]:	她弟弟	在	哪儿?

A

1. Is Ms. Ding, the teacher [= Ding1 Lao3shi1] in?

Ding lǎoshī zài ma? ✓

2. She is not in.

她 不 在. ✗

3. Not all foreign students live in the dormitory.

~~dōu bú~~ liúxuéshēng zhù zai sùshè. ✗
bú dōu

4. May I ask, where does your older brother live? Does he live in China?

qǐngwèn, nǎr nǐ gēge zhù? Tā zhù zài zhōngguó ma? ✓

5. He does not live in China. He lives in France.

Tā bú zhù zài zhōngguó. Tā zhù zài fǎguó. ✓

6. We both live on the third floor. He lives in No. 345; I live in No. 301.

Wǒmen dōu zhù zài sāncéng. Tā zhù zài sānsìwǔ hào. Wǒ zhù zài sānlíngyí hào. ✓

7. Isn't Dr. Xie at the hospital*?

~~Bù~~ Xie dàifu zài ma? ✓
mā

8. Her mother is in the hospital*. [*=supplementary word]

Tā māma ~~shì~~ zai yīyuàn.

9. Could you tell me where is his English dictionary?

qǐngwèn Tā de yīngyǔ cídiǎn zài nǎr. ✓

10. His English dictionary is not here*. His English pictorial is here*.

Tā de yīngyǔ cídiǎn ~~bu shì~~ zhèr. Tā de yīngyǔ huàbào shì zhèr.
zài

Exercise V (Cont.)

B. 翻译 Translation: Apply the illustrated pattern to translate the sentences into Chinese.

Pattern # 13: Position of Time-word

		(a) **Subject**	**at this time**	**<neg.>**	**is in this state.**
		NP	Time-word		Predicate
[Example]:		谢老师	现在		在宿舍.
		(b) **At this time**	**the subject**	**<neg.>**	**is in this state.**
		Time-word	NP		Predicate
[Example]:		现在	他弟弟	不	学习英语.

1. Where is he now?

2. Thank you. I don't want to drink [use "I don't drink"] tea right now.

3. He is not a teacher. He is a student now.

4. Her older brother is currently studying Chinese.

5. The doctor is very busy at this moment.

6. These days, are you using the Chinese dictionary often?

7. Who lives in No. 514 these days?

8. The exchange students are now studying in our dormitory.

9. Do you use the world* atlas* now? [*=supplementary word. Also, you may use the same Chinese word for "map" and "atlas."]

10. Now he often goes to see his girl friend.

Exercise V (Cont.)

C. 翻译 **Translation**: Apply the illustrated pattern to translate the sentences into Chinese.

Pattern # 14: Narrative Sentence: Using verb-of-motion, place word, and verb-of-action to describe motion, destination and purpose.

	Someone NP - person	**comes /goes to** \<neg> V-motion	**this place** NP -place	**to do this.** V-act+Obj:NP
[Example]:	他	去	宿舍	看 朋友.

1. He goes to the Foreign Language Institute to study French.

2. His girlfriend does not go to his dormitory to see him.

3. Where should we go to have some tea? [= Where do we go...?]

4. Is your younger brother going to China to study Chinese?

5. I often go to my friend's dorm to use his Chinese dictionary.

6. Her father often goes to the hospital* to see the doctor. [*=supplementary word]

7. She is now going to the Medical College [=yi1xue2yuan4] to return the books.

8. She is now going to Room 698 to see a friend.

9. Who's going to the Foreign Language Institute to welcome the exchange students?

10. Are you all going to Ding Yun's dormitory to thank her?

Exercise V (Cont.)

D. 词序 Word Order: Rearrange the elements in each entry to make a grammatical sentence.

1. 1 我   3 不   5 词典   4 用   2 现在

2. 3 丁云 (Ding Yun)   4 画报   1 他   2 还

3. 4 你   1 我   3 宿舍   2 住   5 呢

4. 3 朋友   2 的   1 帕兰卡 (Palanka)   4 不   6 画报   5 看

5. 1 学生   6 外语学院   5 的   2 都   4 这儿   3 在

6. 4 汉语   5 老师   2 认识   1 谁   3 他们的

7. 1 他们   5 我的   7 朋友   6 好   4 是   3 都   2 也

8. 1 他   5 书   6 哪儿   4 还   2 去

9. 你   呢   4 喝茶   2 现在   3 去   1 我们
   5   6

10. 6 汉语   2 女朋友   1 车大夫的   5 学习   3 去   4 中 (Zhong1)国

Exercise V (Cont.)

11/18/19

E. 用词 Choice of Words: Choose the most appropriate word or phrase from the list to complete a grammatical sentence.

1. 请问, 厕所(ce4suo3)* ___b___ 哪儿? [*=supplementary word]
   (a) 去   (b) 在   (c) 是

2. 你现在 ___c___ 画报吗?
   (a) 什么   (b) 用   (c) 看

3. 我们常去外语学院 ___b___.
   (a) 朋友   (b) 学习   (c) 英语

4. 古波(Gubo) ___c___ 医院(yi1yuan4)* 看大夫.
   (a) 朋友   (b) 现在   (c) 去

5. 我认识古波, 我也 ___a___ 帕兰卡(Palanka).
   (a) 认识   (b) 朋友   (c) 看

6. 他 ___a___ 不喝茶.
   (a) 现在   (b) 去   (c) 宿舍

7. 您去 ___b___ 看朋友?
   (a) 现在   (b) 哪儿   (c) 什么

8. 他们都是 ___a___ 大夫.
   (a) 很好   (b) 很好的   (c) 认识

9. ___a___ 我们去宿舍看她.
   (a) 现在   (b) 学生   (c) 谁

10. ___b___ 看画报.
   (a) 不   (b) 请   (c) 什么   A

Exercise V (Cont.)

F. 问答 Questions: Answer the following questions according to facts of your real life and the information provided in the lessons.

1. 外语学院的学生都住宿舍吗？老师呢？

2. 你住在宿舍吗？你住多少号？你朋友住哪儿？

3. 谁是古波(Gubo) 的女朋友？她是哪国人？

4. 他们都学习汉语吗？

5. 他们常用汉语词典吗？你呢？

6. 他们的老师是哪国人？他姓什么？

7. 他是很好的汉语老师吗？

8. 丁云(Ding Yun) 是谁？她认识帕兰卡(Palanka) 吗？

9. 丁云也学习汉语吗？ [You may also try to answer this question: 英语呢？]

10. 帕兰卡常去哪儿看丁云？

Exercise VI
(Review: Lessons 7-12)

A. 用词 **Choice of Words**: Fill in each blank with an appropriate Chinese character to make each entry a grammatical sentence.

Note: It is possible that there are more than one correct answers.

1. 谁 _zhu (zai)_ 六二五号?

2. _xianzai_ 她不 _kan newspaper_ 报. [Hint: What may appear before the subject?]

3. 还 _ni_ 报纸(zhi3)*, 谢谢. [*=supplementary word]
   newspaper

4. 古波(Gubo) _de_ 女朋友住 _nhar_ ?

5. "_Qingg_ 坐, _qing_ 喝茶." "谢谢您." "_Bu keqi_."

6. 请问, 谢先生 _zai_ 吗?
   Mr. kan

7. 请 _wen_, 法语词典 _zai_ 哪儿?

8. 她还你 _shu ma_?

9. _Shei_ 还他画报?

10. 我们老师不 _xing_ 谢. 他 _ye_ 不 _shi_ 法国人.
    fagou ren

27

Exercise VI (Cont.)

B. 作文 Composition: (Part 1)

Write a passage about a series of things you plan to do, using the word 看 in each
sentence. As you know, the word 看 may be used for the meaning of "looking at,"
"visiting (someone)," "reading" (a newspaper, magazine/ pictorial, or a book), etc.

C. 作文 Composition (Part 2):

Are you curious about something? Ask questions and find out information about
them. Write a series of questions you may ask to find out information about two or
three different things. Of course, interrogative words such as 什么, 谁, 谁的,
哪儿, 吗, 呢, etc. are useful here.

Exercise VI (Cont.)

D. 作文 Composition (Part 3):

Write a dialogue between you and a friend who came to your place to visit. For example, you might start by greeting her at the door, asking her to come in and offering her something to drink. Later you might be discussing your study and the well being of your family members.

Pàlánkǎ: Sī Tíng, nǐ hǎo.

Lǔ Sī Tíng: nǐ hǎo, qǐng jìn. Qǐng zuò. Qǐng hē chá

Pàlánkǎ: Xièxie.

Lǔ Sī Tíng: Nǐ māma hǎo ma?

Pàlánkǎ: Wǒ māma hěn hǎo, nǐ māma ne?

Lǔ Sī Tíng: Wǒ māma bù hǎo. Tā hěn máng.

Pàlánkǎ: Nǐ xuéxí nǎ wàiyǔ?

Lǔ Sī Tíng: Wǒ xuéxí Hànyǔ, yě xuéxí Fǎyǔ, nǐ ne?

Pàlánkǎ: Wǒ xuéxí Déyǔ.

Lǔ Sī Tíng: Nǐ shì Dīng Yún hěn hǎo de péngyou ma?

Pàlánkǎ: Shì, wǒmen shì hěn hǎo de péngyou.

Lǔ Sī Tíng: Zàijiàn.

Pàlánkǎ: Zàijiàn.

A+

E. 用词 Choice of Words: Write down the appropriate expression for each of the following occasions.

1. You are a polite person and you want to ask a question. What do you say before actually stating our question.

    qǐngwèn.

2. What do you say to indicate your gratitude?

    xièxie

3. When someone shows her gratitude to you, what do you say?

    bù kèqi

Exercise VII
(Lesson 13)

A. 翻译 **Translation**: Apply the illustrated pattern to translate the sentences into Chinese.

Pattern #15: **Interrogative Sentence**: Using "V + Neg. V" structure to form a question.

	Subject	Predicate			
	NP	V_a-state	+	Neg. V_a	
	NP	V_b-id	+	Neg. V_b	+ NP
	NP	V_c-act	+	Neg. V_c	+ Object
	NP	V_d-motion	+	Neg. V_d	+ NP-place
[Example]:	您	忙		不忙？	
	你朋友	姓		不姓	谢？
	他	吸		不吸	烟？
	他们	去		不去	外语学院？

1. Is Dr. Xie busy?

Xie dàifu máng bù máng?

2. Are you going to the store?

Nǐ qù bù qù shāngdiàn?

3. Is his girl friend's name Gu Lanlan? [Do you know how to write the characters for Gu Lanlan?]

Tā de nǚ péngyou xìng bù xìng Gu Lanlan?

4. Is her map of China (a) good (one)?

Tā de zhōngguó dìtú hǎo bù hǎo?

5. Are you studying Chinese?

Nǐ xuéxí bù xuéxí hànyǔ?

6. Is her older brother a student?   shì bù shì

Tā de gēge xuésheng bù xuésheng?

7. Are you buying any paper? (Are you) buying any pens/pencils?

Nǐ mǎi bù mai zhǐ? Nǐ mǎi bù mǎi bǐ?

8. Is her boyfriend coming?

Tā de nán péngyou lái bù lái?

9. Does he speak Chinese?

Tā shuō bù shuō hànyǔ?

10. Are you going to the dormitory to see Mr. Ding, the teacher [= Ding1 Lao3shi1] ?

Nǐ qù bù qù sùshè kàn xiānsheng Dīng lǎoshī?

30

Exercise VII (Cont.)

B. 词序 Word Order: Rearrange the elements in each entry to make a grammatical sentence.

1. 你   王(Wang2)老师   认识   不认识

2. 你   纸   不买   买   请问

3. 她   他的   是   朋友   女   不是

4. 商店   笔   去   买   谁

5. 什么   弟弟   名字   她   叫

6. 古波(Gubo)   学   汉语   都   和   帕兰卡(Panlanka)

7. 词典   英语   用   她   不   常

8. 介绍   我   来   一下儿

9. 哪儿   你   去   喂

10. 吗   他们   谢英   不   认识   都

Exercise VII (Cont.)

C. 用词 Choice of Words: Fill in the blanks with appropriate words, using one character for each blank.

Note: Review the "V + Neg. V" are other interrogative sentence patters. Also review the new words of this lesson. Remember that each exercise is meant to help you review patterns vocabulary already studied.

1. 您认识 _bu_ _renshi_ 车大夫？

2. 她弟弟说 _bu_ _shuo_ 汉语？

3. 丁云(Ding Yun) _de_ 朋友 _zai_ 不在宿舍？

4. 你们 _xue_ 不学习法语吗？

5. 他们 _huanying_ 不欢迎我？

6. 你们 _qu_ _bu_ _qu_ 商店？ (Are you going to the store?)

7. "他爸爸来 _bu_ _lai_ ？" "他来."

8. "你们买 _bu_ _mai_ ？" "我们买笔 _he_ 纸."

9. 她男朋友 _是_ 英国人吗？

10. 他姓 _Qubo_ ？ (他) 叫什么 _中_ _国_ ？

Exercise VII (Cont.)

D. 问答 Questions: Answer the following questions according to the information provided in the lesson and your own real-life situation.

1. 帕兰卡(Palanka) 的男朋友叫什么名字？

2. 古波(Gubo) 是不是中(Zhong1)国人？

3. 古波和帕兰卡去哪儿？

4. 他们去那儿*买什么？丁云(Ding Yun) 呢？[*=supplementary word]

5. 谁学习汉语？

6. 丁云是不是学生？

7. 她学不学英语？

8. 她认识不认识古波？

9. 你常说汉语吗？你用不用汉语词典？

10. 你看不看报？你看不看法语报？

Exercise VIII
(Lessons 14)

A. 翻译 **Translation**: Apply the illustrated pattern to translate the sentences into Chinese.

Pattern # 16: **Ascriptive Sentence**: Using Verb-of-possession/existence 有 and its negative form 没有 to indicate possession or existence, or the negation of such.

	Someone/ some place	**(does not)**	**have**	**this**.
	NP - person/place	<Neg.没>	有	NP
[Example]:	帕兰卡 (Palanka)		有	汉语词典.
	银行 (现在)	没	有	人.

1. We all have a Chinese dictionary.

2. Does Ding Yun have a boyfriend? [Use 吗.]

3. Does your French language teacher have a spouse? [Use 吗.]

4. They don't have any children.

5. The company's* manager has a car. His wife also has a car. [*=supplementary word]

6. The bookstore does not have Chinese newspapers.

7. Her child has no friends.

8. Neither of us has older sisters.

9. There are not any good doctors in the hospital*.

10. There are no exchange students in the Foreign Language Institute.

Exercise VIII (Cont.)

B. 翻译 Translation: Apply the illustrated pattern to translate the sentences into Chinese.

Pattern # 17: **Interrogative Sentence**: Using 有没有 to inquire about possession or existence.

	This person / This place	**has / does not have**	**this.**
	NP - person/place	V + Neg. V 有没有	NP
[Examples]:	您	有没有	笔?
	宿舍	有没有	人?

1. Does she have a husband?

2. Do they have any children?

3. Are there any female doctors in the hospital*?

4. Do you have any sisters or brothers?

5. Are there any male employees* in the bank?

6. Does the college/university have a bookstore?

7. Are there foreign books in the bookstore?

8. Do they have a good French dictionary?

9. Does your friend have a family?

10. Does Dr. Gu have a younger sister?

Exercise VIII (Cont.)

C. 翻译 Translation: Apply the illustrated pattern to translate the sentences into Chinese.

Pattern # 18: **Narrative Sentence:** Using <u>Co-verb 在 + V-of-action (+obj.)</u> to inform the location of an event.

	<u>Someone</u>	<u>at</u>	<u>this place</u>	<u>does this.</u>
	NP - person	Co-verb 在	NP - place	V-act (+Obj:NP)
[Example]:	我姐姐	在	宿舍	看 书.

1. He is reading a newspaper in the Foreign Language Institute.

2. Where do you buy pens/pencils?

3. She works at home.

4. My brother and his girlfriend both work in the bookstore.

5. Who works at the bank?

6. Ding Yun is buying a map at the bookstore.

7. What is her younger sister buying at the store?

8. She is at home writing letters.

9. Where do his children go to school [= study]?

10. What kind of work do you do at the post office*?

Exercise VIII (Cont.)

D. 翻译 Translation: Apply the illustrated pattern to translate the sentences into Chinese.

Pattern # 19: **Narrative Sentence**: Using the Co-verb 给 to indicate "favor" or "offering."

	Someone	**for / to someone else**	**does**	**something**.
	NP-person	Co-verb 给 + NP-person	V-act +	Obj.: NP
[Example]:	我	给　　我姐姐	写	信.

> **Note**: 给 may also be used to mean "on behalf of," "for the sake of," and "for the benefit of."

Pattern #20: **Narrative Sentence**: Using the Verb-of-action 说 or 告诉 to reiterate a statement.

Someone	**state / relates to someone else**	**this information**.
NP-person	V-act 说 / 告诉 + NP-person	Statement
她	说	她去买书.
谢友学	告诉　　我	车大夫很忙.

1. I am writing to my family.

2. Dr. Xie bought us the newspaper.

3. Her boy friend is returning the book for her.

4. Mr. Che, the teacher, [= Che1 Lao3shi1] introduced us to each other.

5. She told me she is homesick.

6. He says that you (plural) are good friends.

7. My older brother tells us that she misses home very much.

8. I told him I work for a bank.

9. He asked me where the bank is.

10. His mother is buying a pen for him.

Exercise VIII (Cont.)

E. 词序 Word Order: Rearrange the elements in each entry to make a grammatical sentence.

1. 他　　孩子　　没有

2. 在　　书店　　他爱人　　不　　工作

3. 妹妹　　谢大夫　　没有　　有

4. 我　　写信　　给　　常　　请(你)

5. 银行　　女朋友　　她　　是　　经理(jing1li3)*　　的

6. 他　　他　　说　　工作　　邮局(you2ju2)*　　在

7. 告诉　　我　　我　　他　　喝茶　　不

8. 我　　我朋友　　写信　　给　　常

9. 你　　他们　　请　　问　　好

10. 姐姐　　有　　没有　　你

Exercise VIII (Cont.)

F. 用词 Choice of Words: Fill in each blank with an appropriate character to make grammatical sentences.

1. 他 _____ 什么工作? (What does he do?)

2. 留学生都很 _____ 家. (... homesick.)

3. 他姐姐在 _____ _____ 工作?

4. 我常 _____ 我朋友 _____ 信.

5. 您有 _____ _____ 妹妹?

6. 他 _____ _____ 我他 _____ 想他妈妈.

7. 她 _____ 我书店有 _____ _____ 法语书. (She asks me if there is....)

8. 请 _____ 您爸爸妈妈好.

9. 她爱人不 _____ 外语学院 _____ _____ 英语.

10. 他 _____ 他哥哥常买书 _____ 他.

Exercise VIII (Cont.)

G. 问答 **Questions:** Answer the questions according to the information provided in the lessons.

1. 丁云 (Ding Yun) 想不想家？想不想她爸爸妈妈？

2. 她也想她男朋友吗？

3. 丁云有没有姐姐妹妹？她有没有哥哥弟弟？

4. 她姐姐在哪儿工作？

5. 丁云的姐姐有没有孩子？

6. 谁在医院(yi1yuan4)* 工作？

7. 他作什么工作？

8. 丁云常给她姐姐写信吗？

9. 你想丁云也常给她爸爸妈妈, 她男朋友写信吗？

10. 丁云在哪儿学习？她学习什么？

Exercise IX
(Lessons 15)

A. 翻译 **Translation**: Apply the illustrated pattern to translate the sentences into Chinese.

Pattern #21: Expression of Quantity: <Number> + <Measure Word>

	... this many	units of	people / things ...
	Adj. - Number	Measure-word	NP - person/thing
[Examples]:	三	本 *ben*	书
	六	个 *ge*	学生

Pattern #22: Interrogative Sentence: Using Question-word 几/多少 to inquire about quantity.

	... how much / how many	units of	people / thing ...
	Q-word 几	Measure-word	NP - person/thing
	Q-word 多少	(Measure-word)	NP - person/thing
[Examples]:	几 *ji*	本 *ben*	杂志
	多少 *duoshu* / *duoshao*	(个) *ge*	老师

A

1. Mr. Wang, the teacher [= Wang2 Lao3shi1] has one older brother and one younger sister.

Wáng lǎoshī yǒu yí gè gēge, yí ge mèimei

2. The Foreign Language Institute has five teachers and forty-eight students.

wàiyǔ xuéyuàn yǒu wǔ ge laoshi, sì shí bā gè

3. He now knows ninety-four Chinese characters.

Tā rènshi jiǔ shí sì gè hànzi

4. She has three Chinese friends. xuésheng

Tā yǒu san ge zhongguo pengyou

5. I'll buy one world atlas and three magazines.

Wǒ mai yi běn shì jiè dìtu he san běn zashi

6. The library has three reading rooms.

Túshūguǎn yǒu san ge yuèlǎnshi

7. How many departments are there in the Foreign Language Institute?

duoshao xì you zai wàiyǔ xuéyuàn?

8. May I ask, how many students are there in the Chinese Department?

Qing wen, duoshao xuésheng zai zhōngwénxi?

9. How many English and French language teachers do you have?

Nǐ yǒu duoshao yingyu he fayu laoshi?

10. How many Chinese language grammar books are you buying?

Nǐ mai duoshao zhongwén yǔfǎ shu?

41

Exercise IX (Cont.)

B. 翻译 Translation: Apply the illustrated pattern to translate the sentences into Chinese.

Pattern #23: **Types of modifiers**

Modifier		Key-word/phrase/clause
Noun - word/phrase/clause	(英国)	Noun (人)
Adj. - word/phrase/clause	(新)	Noun (车)
Adv. - word/phrase/clause	(很)	Adj. (好)
Adv. - word/phrase/clause	(常)	Verb (买)
Adv. - word/phrase/clause	(都)	Adv. (很)...
Adv. - word/phrase/clause	(常)	Clause (在阅览室看书)

1. This is a <u>new</u> book.

2. I <u>often</u> buy <u>Chinese</u> magazines.

3. Are <u>new</u> cars <u>all</u> <u>very</u> <u>good</u>?

4. They <u>both</u> have <u>girl</u> friends.

5. We learn <u>from each other</u> [= mutually].

6. He does <u>not often</u> write to his mother.

7. <u>New</u> <u>American</u> cars are <u>not</u> <u>all</u> good.

8. I <u>often</u> drink <u>English</u> tea at the <u>new</u> shop.

9. He often buys French newspapers at the Student Bookstore.

10. Gubo is a <u>very good</u> friend of his. Palanka is <u>also</u> a <u>good</u> friend <u>of his</u>.

Exercise IX (Cont.)

C. 翻译 Translation: Apply the illustrated pattern to translate the sentences into Chinese.

Pattern #24: **Compound Sentence**: Using Parallel Clauses to present similar situations.

	A	**does this,**	**B**	**also**	**does this.**
	Subj. 1	Pred.	Subj. 2	也	Pred.
	NP1	V + Obj.	NP2	也	V + Obj.
[Example]:	他	学习汉语,	他哥哥	也	学习汉语.

	A	**does this,**	**A**	**also**	**does that.**
	Subj. 1	Pred.	Subj. 2	也	Pred.
	NP1	V + Obj.	NP2	也	V + Obj.
[Example]:	他	看杂志,	他	也	看报.

1. He doesn't drink tea. I don't, either.

   Tā bù hē chá, Wǒ yě bù hē chá.

2. He teaches Chinese. He also studies French.

   Tā jiāo hànyǔ, Tā yě xué fàyǔ.

3. Mr. Xie teaches them characters. He also teaches grammar.

   Mr. Xie jiāo tāmen hànzì, Ta ye jiāo yǔfǎ.

4. She often writes to me. She also often writes to my younger brother.

   Tā cháng xiě xìn gěi wǒ. Tā ye cháng xiě xìn gěi wǒ didi.
   Tā yě cháng gěi wǒ didi xiě xìn.

5. They don't often buy magazines. They also don't buy newspapers.

   Tāmen bù cháng mǎi zázhì. Tāmen yě bù mǎi bào.

6. There are often students in the new reading room. The old [=lao3] reading room often has students, too.

7. She often buys books for him. She also teaches him new Chinese characters.

   Tā cháng gěi tā mǎi shū. Tā yě gěi tā jiāo xīn hànzì.

8. The Chinese Department has five exchange students. So does the French Department.

   Hànyǔ xì yǒu wǔ ge liúxuéshēng. Fǎyǔ yě yǒu.

9. He went to the library to read magazines and also to borrow* some books.

   Ta qù túshūguǎn kan zazhi, yě jiè shu.

10. I have three dictionaries. I also have twenty-five Chinese books.

    Wǒ yǒu sān běn cídiǎn. Wǒ yě yǒu èrshí wǔ běn hànyǔ shu.

43

Exercise IX (Cont.)

D. 词序 Word Order: Rearrange the elements in each entry to make a grammatical sentence.

1. 学生   中文系   九十七   有   个

2. 我们   系   老师   十   个   有

3. 我们   学习   互相

4. 口语   我们   教   谢老师

5. 你们   谁   语法   教

6. 杂志   法文   没有   阅览室

7. 我   我   中文   法文   学习   学习   也

8. 几个   外国   朋友   有   你

9. 我   他   看   画报   和   都

10. 几   词典   汉语   本   图书馆   有

Exercise IX (Cont.)

E. 用词 Choice of Words: Choose the most appropriate word or phrase from the list.

1. 外语学院 ___ c ___ 多少学生?
    (a) 是   (b) 在   (c) 有

2. 王(Wang) 老师有一 ___ a ___ 女孩子.
    (a) 个   (b) 本   (c) 没
         of   ben

3. 新阅览室有六 ___ b ___ 汉语词典.
    (a) 个   (b) 本 book measurement   (c) (leave it blank)

4. 古波(Gubo)学习汉语, 帕兰卡(Palanka) ___ c ___ 学习汉语.
    (a) 还   (b) 和   (c) 也

5. 谢大夫看报, 他 ___ a ___ 写信.
    (a) 也   (b) 和   (c) 常

6. 她教我们汉字, ___ c ___ 我们语法.
    (a) 也她教   (b) 和她教   (c) 她也教

7. 书店有中文报, ___ c ___ 中文杂志.
    (a) 也   (b) 和   (c) 有也
         ye   he   you ye

8. 她去书店买笔, 买纸, ___ c ___ 报.
    (a) 也   (b) 和   (c) 也买
                                        ye mai

because there is a comma, no "和" with he.

he

9. 请问, 您有 ___ c ___ 语法书?
    (a) 三本   (b) 多少个   (c) 几本

10. 中文系有 ___ b ___ 留学生?
    (a) 几   (b) 多少   (c) 十二

45

Exercise IX (Cont.)

F. 问答 **Questions:** Answer the following questions according to your real-life situations.

1. 请问，你们中文系有多少学生？

2. 中文系有没有中国老师？

3. 谁教你们语法？汉字呢？

4. 请问，哪儿有中文画报？

5. 那儿也有中文杂志吗？

6. 外语学院的阅览室有多少法文书？法文画报呢？

7. 你有没有哥哥弟弟姐姐妹妹？有几个？

8. 你和谁去书店？

9. 你们去买什么？

10. 你们图书馆有什么书？

1, 2, 3, 4

Exercise X
(Lesson 16)

A. 翻译 Translation: Apply the illustrated pattern to translate the sentences into Chinese.

Pattern #25: **Ascriptive Sentence**: Using 的 to indicate ownership, condition, or color.

	This person/thing	**is**	**of this kind (person/thing)**
	Modifier + N	V-id + (的) +	(N)
[Examples]:	这条裙子	是　新的	(裙子).
	那个车	是　她的/红的	(车).

Note: This type of sentence is used to <u>describe</u> the condition or other qualities such as color and ownership of the subject. It is also useful for making comparison and contrast when parallel clauses are used. Now, compare it with the following sentences of slightly different structures:

(a)　"这是一条新裙子."　(To identify the subject.)

(b)　"这条裙子很新."　(To comment on the subject.)

Also Note: In the predicate, the noun after 的 is generally omitted.

1. This skirt is not a new one.

Zhe tiao qunzi bushi xinde

2. This is his shirt; this shirt is his.

Zhe shi ta de chenshan.. zhe jian chemshan shi ta de

3. Both her skirt and her shirt are new.

Ta de qunzi he chenshan duo shi xin de

4. My shirt is white and his is blue.

wo de chenshan shi baide. Ta de shi lan de.

5. This green skirt is my older sister's, not my younger sister's.

Zhe tiao lü qunzi bu shi wo miemied, shi wo jie jie de.

6. This shirt is new. That one is old.

Zhe jian chenshan shi xinde. na jian shi jiu de.

7. This new skirt is hers. That old one is also hers.

Zhe tiao xin qunzi shi ta de. Na tiao jiu de yeshi ta de.

8. Is this green skirt yours? It is very pretty [=hao3kan4].

zhe tiao lü qunzi shi ni de ma? Shi hen haokan de

9. "Whose jacket* is this? Is it yours?" "This one is not mine. That one is." [Reminder: *=supplementary word]

"zhe jian shàngyi shi shei de? Shi ni de?" "zhe bu shi wo de. najian shi wo de"

10. Mine is not new. His is not new, either.

wo de bu shi xinde. Ta de ye bu shi xinde

women dou bu shi xin de

Exercise X (Cont.)

B. 翻译 Translation: Apply the illustrated pattern to translate the sentences into Chinese.

Pattern #26: Narrative Sentence: Using <Co-verb 从> ... <V-motion 来/去>... <V-action> structure to describe movement, destination and purpose.

Someone	**from**	**place 1**	**comes to / goes to**	**place 2**	**to do this.**
NP-person	Co-V 从	NP-place	来 / 去	NP-place	V-act + Obj.
[Example]: 他们	从	宿舍	去	图书馆	还 书.

1. He is going from his house to the theatre*.

2. He is going to the theatre* to buy tickets.

3. He goes from his house to the bookstore to buy (some) books for his parents.

4. I am going to the store to buy two shirts and one skirt for my younger sister.

5. They are coming to my dormitory to see my new shirts.

6. They are going from here to the Chinese (materials) reading room.

7. Her boyfriend is coming to her house from France this evening.

8. My friend and I are going there to look for that magazine now.

9. [This] evening, we are going to the Chinese Language Institute to see a Beijing Opera.

10. Who is going there to look for him?

Exercise X (Cont.)

C. 词序 Word order: Rearrange the elements of each entry to make a grammatical sentence.

1. 京剧　　看　　　　去　　　　丁教授

2. 我们　　他　　　　票　　　　京剧　　　两张　　　给

3. 我们　　我们家　　去　　　　从　　　　剧场*　　京剧　　看

4. 宿舍　　图书馆　　去　　　　从　　　　他们　　　还　　　书

5. 什么　　您　　　　找　　　　那儿　　　去

6. 我的　　是　　　　裙子　　　这　　　　条

7. 新　　　件　　　　衬衫　　　是　　　　那　　　　的

8. 她　　　新　　　　的　　　　穿　　　　裙子　　　绿

9. 大衣　　太　　　　大　　　　这　　　　件

10. 我们　　看　　　　京剧　　　晚上　　　去

Exercise X (Cont.)

D. 用词 Choice of Words: Fill in the blanks with the most appropriate words, using one character for each blank.

1. 这 ____ 衬衫不是我 ____ . ____ 不是新的.

2. 那 ____ 新 ____ 白裙子是她姐姐 ____ .

3. 我晚上 ____ 这儿 ____ 你家看你.

4. 我不 ____ (wear) 这 ____ 新大衣*,我 ____ 那 ____ 旧 ____ .

5. 他们常常 ____ 宿舍 ____ 书店 ____ 杂志.

6. 他们从 ____ ____ 去剧场* ____ 京剧.

7. 我有两 ____ 票.我们 ____ 看京剧.

8. 他常常从他朋友 ____ 儿来我们 ____ 儿找丁云.

9. 那 ____ 绿衬衫太大,不好,我不 ____ .

10. 那 ____ 书店很大,我们常常去 ____ ____ 买书.

Exercise X (Cont.)

E. 复习 Review: Numbers and Measure Words: Fill in the blanks using the given quantity and proper measure words.

1. _____ _____ 票 (3)

2. _____ _____ 学生 (15)

3. _____ _____ 衬衫 (2)

4. _____ _____ 杂志 (50)

5. _____ _____ 裙子 (4)

6. _____ _____ 哥哥 (3)

7. _____ _____ 书店 (8)

8. _____ _____ 大夫 (12)

9. _____ _____ 银行 (23)

10. _____ _____ 宿舍 (55)

11. _____ _____ 词典 (2)

12. _____ _____ 地图 (10)

13. _____ _____ 大衣 * (5)

14. _____ _____ 中文书 (26)

15. _____ _____ 裤子 (1)

16. _____ _____ 老师 (7)

17. _____ _____ 图书馆 (2)

18. _____ _____ 朋友 (13)

19. _____ _____ 系 (46)

20. _____ _____ 学院 (20)

Exercise X (Cont.)

F. 问答 Answering Questions: Answer the following questions according to the information provided in the lesson and the actual situations about yourself.

1. 王老师给古波两张什么票？

2. 古波和帕兰卡晚上去作什么？他们从哪儿去？

3. 帕兰卡穿哪件衬衫，哪条裙子去？

4. 你有几件衬衫？

5. 帕兰卡有没有白裙子？你呢？

6. 你的上衣*是绿的吗？

7. 你的衬衫都是新的吗？

8. 你妹妹常穿新裙子吗？

9. 你常去你老师家看他吗？

10. 你们去哪儿买笔？从哪儿去？

LU SiTing
5/23/00

Exercise XI (Cont.)

C. 词序 Word order: Rearrange the elements of each entry to make a grammatical sentence.

1. 半④ 点② 四② 下课⑤ 我们①

2. 我② 不③ 看⑤ 京剧⑥ 去④ 晚上①

3. 一刻② 六点① 他⑤ 我③ 等④ 在⑥ 食堂⑦

4. 八点② 二十分③ 上课④ 他们①

5. 以后② 下课① 宿舍⑤ 我③ 回④

6. 电影⑤ 几点③ 的④ 看② 我们①

7. 他① 上课⑤ 常② 坐车③ 去④

8. 去② 咖啡馆④ 我们① 走③

9. 车④ 三点半① 坐③ 去⑥ 我⑤ 图书馆⑦ 的②

10. 我① 我姐姐③ 咖啡⑦ 一起④ 去⑤ 跟② 喝⑥

Exercise XI (Cont.)

D. 用词 Choice of Words: Fill in the blanks with the most appropriate words, using one character for each blank.

1. 我 _____ 我朋友一起 _____ 看电影.

2. 请你六 _____ 半 _____ 宿舍等我.

3. 下课 _____ 后我 _____ 家.

4. 我们 _____ 车 _____ 书店 _____ 书.

5. 他们去 _____ 九点一刻 _____ 电影.

6. 我七 _____ 二十分回宿舍 _____ 信.

7. 我们不 _____ 车去, 我们 _____ 去.

8. 您晚上 _____ 事儿吗? 我 _____ 看您, 好吗?

9. 我八 _____ 钟 _____ 前*没有课.

10. 现在 _____ 五分两 _____ .

Exercise XI
(Lesson 18)

A. 翻译 Translation: Apply the illustrated pattern to translate the sentences into Chinese.

Pattern #28: **Narrative Sentence:** Using the expression "每 + Measure-word... (都)" to indicate routine or persistent activities and situations.

Someone	**everyday / every time-unit**	**does this.**
Subj.: person <-->	每(+) + Time unit	(都) Predicate
[Examples]: 他	每天	六点钟起床.
古波	每天上午	都 去看他女朋友.

Pattern #29: **Narrative Sentence:** Using the expression "有时候" to indicate occasional events.

Occasionally	**someone**	**does this.**
有时候 <-->	Subj.: person	Predicate
[Example]: 有时候	我们	在宿舍看电影.

Note: **A <--> B** indicates that the positions of A and B may be switched.
These two patterns, #28 and #29, may also be applied to other situations with non-personal subjects. For example: "图书馆每天都有人." "有时候问题很多." In Pattern #28, with the word "都" the sentence emphasizes the consistency of an action. Without the word "都" the sentence refers to a normal daily routine.

1. I have classes every morning.   2. She sometimes has classes in the afternoon too.

3. He always [=everyday, consistently] takes the bus to come here.

4. She goes to the college every day at a quarter past seven.

5. Every day after class she goes to the library to read.

6. Sometimes she does not eat in the dining hall.

7. Every evening [= Everyday's evening] after dinner she writes letter to her parents.

8. Occasionally she goes to see a movie with her friends.

9. Occasionally she also goes to the teacher's house to ask questions.

10. He sometimes eats after 6:00 p.m. and sometimes before* 6:00 p.m. [*=supplementary word]

Exercise XII (Cont.)

B. 词序 Word order: Rearrange the elements of each entry to make a grammatical sentence.

1. 你　　　起床　　　几点钟　　　每天

2. 我们　　课　　　有　　　　每天　　　都

3. 他　　　都　　　很多　　　有　　　　问题　　　每天

4. 以后　　下课　　食堂　　　去　　　　吃饭　　　他们

5. 他们　　词典　　两本　　　每个人 * (each person)　　有

6. 有　　　每个系 * (each department)　　　都　　中国留学生　　　文学院

7. 每天　　以后　　十二点　　睡觉　　　她

8. 上午　　问题　　问　　　我　　　　那儿　　　老师　　　去

9. 她　　　这儿　　北京 *　　学习　　　汉语　　　去　　　从

10. 我　　有时候　　有时候　　在宿舍　　休息　　　在阅览室　看报

Exercise XII (Cont.)

C. 用词 Choice of Words: Fill in the blanks with the most appropriate words, using one character for each blank.

1. 她 _____ 天 (every day) 六点半_____ 床 (gets up) .

2. 他们每天 _____ 有中文课 .

3. 他的每件大衣 (*every overcoat) _____ 是黑的 .

4. 我 每_____ 晚上 _____ 在图书馆看书 .

5. 谢老师给我们 _____ 个学生两 _____ 中文杂志 .

6. 我有时候十一点半睡觉, _____ _____ _____ 十二点(钟) _____ _____ .

7. 他常去 _____ 那儿 _____ 问题 ?

8. 我 _____ 王老师两 _____ 问题 .

9. 吃饭 _____ _____ 我想 _____ 他一起 _____ 阅览室 _____ 报 .

10. 晚上我有时候跟朋友 _____ _____ 去看电影, _____ _____ _____
    在宿舍学习 .

Exercise XII (Cont.)

D. 问答 Answering Questions: Answer the following questions according to the information given in the textbook.

1. 丁云是哪个系的学生？

2. 他们系有很多中国留学生吗？

3. 英语系的中国留学生都住在哪儿？

4. 丁云每天几点钟起床？几点钟睡觉？

5. 她每天都有课吗？

6. 她几点上课？几点下课？

7. 她在哪儿吃饭？

8. 她几点去阅览室看报？

9. 她下午还作什么？

10. 她晚上作什么？

Christine Cohen
2/28/00   M. Chu

Bu Dong!!!

Exercise XIII
(Review L. 13-18)

A. 用词 Choice of Words: Fill in the blanks with the most appropriate words, using one character for each blank.

1. "_Qing_ 问,古波 _zai_ 哪儿?" "他 ~~zai~~ 丁云 ~~nar~~."

2. 他 ~~zu~~ 宿舍 _gei_ 朋友 _xie_ 信.

3. 你们认识 _bu ren shi_ 张老师?" "我们 _dou_ 不认识他."

4. "他去 _nar_ 还书?" "他去帕兰卡 _jia_ 还书."

5. 他们 _cong_ 学院去商店 _mai_ 什么?

6. 你跟 _ta_ 一起去 _kan_ 京剧?你们 _zuo_ 车去吗?

7. "你买 _shenme_?" "我 _mai_ 两 _jian_ 衬衫,一 _tiao_ 裙子,两 _ben_ 书,_he_ 三 _zhang_ 京剧票."

8. 下午 _xia_ 课 _yi_ 后我 ~~ye~~ 跟朋友 _yi qi_ 去咖啡 _guan_ 喝咖啡.晚上我 _you shi hou_ 去图书馆 _kan shu_ 有时候 _zai_ 家休息.

9. 晚上我们 _qu_ 看七 _dian_ 半 _de_ 电影.你 _ye_ _qu_ _ma_?

10. "_Qing_ 问,现在 _ji dian_?" "_cha_ 十 _fen_ 两点."

63

Exercise XIII (Cont.)

B. 作文 **Composition:** Write a series of questions asking your friend about the Chinese department of his/her school.

C. 作文 **Composition:** Write a passage about your schedule for a normal school day.

Exercise XIII (Cont.)

D. 作文 Composition: A Note to a Blind Date: Your good friend Randy has set up a blind date for you but it's up to you to decide on the details. So, you are going to ask Randy to give a note to your blind date. In the note you are going to ask your date to meet you at a certain time and a certain place. You are also going to tell your date what kind of car you will be driving, what clothes you will be wearing, and may be even something you are going to carry with you just to further help your date to identify you. (Of course, this may also be used as a note to prepare yourself for a telephone conversation with your date before you meet.)

2/29/00

Exercise XIV
(Lesson 19)

A. 翻译 **Translation**: Apply the illustrated pattern to translate the sentences into Chinese.

Pattern #30b: **Interrogative Sentence:** Using <是... 还是...> structure to inquire about choices or relative degree -- on the predicate.

+	**The subject**	**is**	**(doing / like) this**	**or**	**(doing/like) that?**
	Subj.	(是)	Pred. A	还是	Pred. B
[Examples]:	他	是	学生	还是	老师?
	你们	(是)	去看电影	还是	回宿舍?
请告诉我	她	(是)	三点(钟)来	还是	四点(钟)

1. Do you like classical music or popular music.

    Ni xihuan gudian yinyuè haishi xihuang xiandai yinyuè?

2. Do you like to drink jasmine tea or black tea?

    Ni xihuan he huā chá haishi he hong cha?
    xihuan

3. Is this a French folk song or a German [=De2guo2 德国] folk songs?

    Zhe shi faguo de minge haishi Deguo de minge?

4. Does your friend live in a dormitory or live at home?

    Ni de pengyou zu zai sushe haishi zu zai jia?

5. I don't know whether he wants a glass of beer or a bottle of beer.

    Wǒ bú zhēdào Ta yao yibēi pijiu haishi yao yiping pijiu.

6. Was the attendant at the Coffee Shop male or female?

    Kafeiguan de fuwuyuan shi nan haishi nu?

7. Do you want to buy apples* or oranges? [*=supplementary word]

    Ni yao u mai pingguo haishi guzi, P?

8. Do you prefer to sing songs or listen to them [=to listen to songs]?

    Ni xihuan chang ger haishi ting ger?

9. Is the classical music dictionary in the library or at the reading room?

    gudian yinyue de cidian zai tushuguan haishi zai yuelanshi?

10. Is your teacher's family name Bai or Zhang?

    Ni de laoshi de xingshi Bai haishi Zhang?

66

Christine Jabins 3/6/00 M. Chu

Exercise XIV (Cont.)

B. 翻译 **Translation**: Apply the illustrated pattern to translate the sentences into Chinese.

Pattern #30b: **Interrogative Sentence**: Using <是... 还是...> structure to inquire about choices or relative degree -- on the subject.

	Is	**A (doing this/ more like this) or**		**B doing this / more like this**?
	(是)	Subj. 1 (Pred.)	还是	Subj. 2. Pred.
[Examples]:	是	你	还是	你朋友去买票?
		大夫 忙	还是	老师 忙?

1. Is the green shirt or the white shirt newer?

shi lu de chenshen haishi bai de xine?   *xin tai*   *xinde?*

2. Are you or your friend ordering an orange juice?

Shi ni haishi ni pengyou gao juzishuy?

3. Is French wine* or American wine* tastier?

Shi fagvo Jiu haishi meiguo Jiu gen hao?   *Jiu*

4. Is Mr. Xie [=Xie4 Lao3shi1] or Mrs. Gu [=Gu3 Lao3shi1] teaching you Chinese grammar?

Shi xie Laoshi haishi Gu Laoshi Jiao nim zhongwen yufa?

5. Which do you think are more pleasant to listen to, folk songs or modern popular songs?

Ni xihuan ting minge haishi ting xiandai ge?

6. Is her older sister or her younger sister prettier?

Shi Ta jiejie geng piaoliang haishi Ta meimei geng piaoliang?

7. Who do you think is better looking, the book shop attendant or the coffee shop attendant?

Shi shudian de fuwuyuan haishi kafeiguan de fuwuyuan geng piaoliang?   *geng piaoliang*

8. Is it going to be Miss Wang or Mr. Ma who teaches us to sing folk songs?

Shi xiaojie wang haishi xiesheng ma jiao women chang minge?   *Wang*   *Ma*

9. Who wants to buy the flower vase* [=bottle], you or your older brother?

shi ni yao mai huar ping
Shi ni haishi ni gege yao mai huar ping?

10. Are you coming to my place to see him or should he go to your house to see you?

Ni lai wo de Jia kan ta haishi Ta qu ni de Jia kan ni?

Exercise XIV (Cont.)

C. 词序 Word order: Rearrange the elements of each entry to make a grammatical sentence.

1. 要   桔子水   杯   一   我

2. 喝   红茶   喜欢   不   你   吗

3. 要   要   红茶   花茶   你   还是

4. 听   喜欢   还是   你们   现代音乐   古典音乐

5. 请   啤酒   一瓶   我   给

6. 我   唱片   两   买   要   张

7. 我   好吗   你   教   中国   民歌   请

8. 在   音乐   宿舍   我们   晚上   听

9. 他   的   听   别

10. 喝   咖啡   中国人   不   都   喜欢

68

[handwritten top:] Xia xingqiliu 是 wo de shengri (san yue shiyi hao) — **M. Chu**

Exercise XV
(Lesson 20)

A. 翻译 Translation: Apply the illustrated pattern to translate the sentences into Chinese.

Pattern #31: Ascriptive Sentence: Using Verb-of-identification to indicate dates and time

(a)	**This date/time**	**is**	**a day/time with this description.**
	Subj.	V-id	Complement
	NP-calendar date/sequential time	是	NP-calendar date/clock time

[Example]: 今天 *(jintian) (today)*　　是　　十一月二十五号. *yue (month)　hao (day of the month)*

(b)	**This date/time**	**is**	**that of this timely event.**
	Subj.	V-id	Complement
	NP-calendar date/sequential time	是	NP-Timely or listed event(s)

[Example]: 下星期四 *xia Thursday*　　是　　他哥哥的生日. *shengri (birthday event)*

(c)	**This event**	**is**	**at this time.**
	Subj.	V-id	Complement
	NP-Event	是/是在	NP-calendar date/clock time

[Example]: 舞会 *wuhui (dance ball)*　　是(在) *zai*　　八点钟. *ba dian*

1. "What's today's date?" [=Today is what month, what day?]　"Today is December 3rd."

Jintian shi shenme yue he ri? shenme (Jintian shi ji yue ji hao)
Jintian shi shier yue san hao.

2. "What day (of the week) is today." [=Today is what day (of the week)?]　"Today is Tuesday."

Jintian shi xingqi ji?　Jintian shi xingqi er.

3. "Is this year's October 1st a Saturday?"　[Can you also answer this question in Chinese?]

Jinnian de shi yue yi hao shi xingqi liu ma?

4. "When is the Department's party [=evening party]?"　"(It) is at 8:30 tonight [=today evening]."

Wanghui ji dian? Wanghui zai jintian wangshang ba dian ban.

5. After Sunday is Monday.

Xingqiri yihou shi xingqi yi.

6. The tutorial class is at 3:15 p.m.

fudou de ke shi xiawu san dian yi ke.

7. Is this year 1993?

Jinnian shi yi jiu jiu san nian ma?

8. Both of their birthdays are in September.

Tamen de shengri dou zai jiu yue.

9. My afternoon class is at 12:20 and his is at 2:00.

Wo xiawu de ke shi shier dian ershi fen.
Ta xiawu de ke shi liang dian.

10. This month is February. Afterwards (it) is March.

Xianzai er yue. Yihou shi san yue.

71

Exercise XV (Cont.)

B. 词序 Word order: Rearrange the elements of each entry to make a grammatical sentence.

1. 有   下午   课   今天   我

2. 我   问题   两个   有

3. 是   十九号   六月   生日   他的

4. 空儿   晚上   今天   我   没有

5. 现在   有事儿   您   吗

6. 很   有意思   学习   语法

7. 舞会   不参加   他   的   中文系

8. 老师   辅导   我们   给   七点钟   晚上

9. 十月   星期四   是   吗   二十七号

10. 一九九五年   不是   十五号   九月   今天

Exercise XV (Cont.)

C. 用词 Choice of Words: Fill in the blanks with the most appropriate words, using one character for each blank.

1. 张老师两点有课 ＿＿＿＿ ＿＿＿＿ 两点半有课？

2. 今天 ＿＿＿＿ 她十八＿＿＿＿ 的生日.

3. 他 ＿＿＿＿ (requests) 老师 ＿＿＿＿ 他们辅导.

4. 我下午没课, 我 ＿＿＿＿ 空儿.

5. 他的同学都不 ＿＿＿＿ ＿＿＿＿ 他 ＿＿＿＿ 的地址.

6. 他的生日是 ＿＿＿＿ 九 ＿＿＿＿ 七 ＿＿＿＿. 今年他二十一 ＿＿＿＿.

7. 星期日我家 ＿＿＿＿ 一个舞会. 欢迎你们 ＿＿＿＿ ＿＿＿＿.

8. 他说舞会 ＿＿＿＿ ＿＿＿＿ 意思. 他不＿＿＿＿ 加.

9. "星期三我 ＿＿＿＿ 你看电影, 你有空儿去吗？" "谢谢你, 我有 ＿＿＿＿ ＿＿＿＿. 我 ＿＿＿＿ ＿＿＿＿ 去."

10. 他九 ＿＿＿＿ 一刻来 ＿＿＿＿ 我们辅导.

73

Exercise XV (Cont.)

D. 问答 Answering Questions: Answer the following questions according to your real-life situations.

1. 今天是几月几号？星期几？ ✓

Jintian shi si yué er hao, xingqiri

2. 请问现在几点？

Xianzai yidian ✓

3. 你的生日是哪一天？你今年的生日是不是在星期六？

wo de shengri shi san yué shi yi hao.
         wo jinnian de shengri shi zai xingqi liu ✓

4. 今天的语法，你有问题吗？

jintian de yufa wo mei you wenti. ✓

5. 你常去听音乐会吗？

wo bu chang qu ting yinyuehui ✓

6. 音乐会有意思吗？

ting yinyue you yisi. ✓

7. 星期日你有空儿吗？

Xingqiri wo mei you kongr. ✓

8. 音乐老师的生日舞会你去不去参加？

wo bu qu canjia yinyue laoshi de shengri ✓
                                          wuhui

9. 你知道不知道那个舞会是哪天？ ✓

wo bu zhidao n

10. 你知道音乐老师家的地址吗？ ✓

Wo bu zhidao yinyué laoshi de dizhi

很好！

Exercise XV (Cont.)

E. 问答 Answering Questions: Answer the following questions based on the illustrated calendar and the real-life situation. The day highlighted is the day when Wang San's younger brother was born.

```
┌─────────────────────────────────────────────┐
│                 1 9 9 2                       │
├─────────────────────────────────────────────┤
│                                         1     │
│   2     3     4     5     6     7     8        │
│   9    10    11    12    13    14   15        │
│  16    17    18    19    20    21   22        │
│  23    24    25    26    27    28   29        │
├─────────────────────────────────────────────┤
│                 February                      │
└─────────────────────────────────────────────┘
```

1. 王三(的)弟弟的生日是几月几号？

2. 王三的弟弟今年几岁？

3. 今年是一九九二年吗？

4. 一九九二年的二月有多少天？一九九三年呢？今年呢？

5. 一九九二年的二月一号是星期几？

6. 今年的二月十号是星期一吗？二十五号呢？

7. 一九九二年的二月有几个星期六？星期天呢？今年呢？

8. 王三弟弟的生日都是在星期六吗？

Exercise XVI
(Lesson 21)

A. 翻译 Translation: Apply the illustrated pattern to translate the sentences into Chinese.

<u>**Pattern #32a:**</u> **Complex Sentence with Clause as Modifier:** To give additional information on the predicate.

> <u>**Note:**</u> This type of sentence may be viewed as combining two sentences of common object.
> <u>Sub-sentence #1</u>: Subj.1+V.1+Obj. 他喜欢喝酒. (He likes to drink wine.)
> <u>Sub-sentence #2</u>: Subj.2+V.2+Obj. 我送他一瓶酒. (I give him a bottle of wine.)
> **New Sentences:**
> Subj. 1 + V.1 + (information from #2) 的 + Obj.
> 他喜欢喝<u>我送他的</u>酒. (He likes to drink the wine that I gave him.)
> Subj. 2 + V.2 + (information from #1) 的 + Obj.
> 我送他一瓶<u>他喜欢喝的</u>酒. (I gave him a bottle of wine that he likes to drink.)

1. We will all attend the dancing party he gives. [Note: to give a party = "kai1 wu3hui4"]

   Women dou canjia   ta kaide wuhui

2. Many people like to read the magazines that the Chinese Reading Room does not have.

   Hen dou ren xihuan kan zhongwen
   Yuelanshi mei you de zazhi

3. Please open the bottle of wine that your friend gave you.

   Qing kai yi ping ni pengyou gei ni de jiu

4. All exchange students from Japan take the English Grammar course taught by Mr. Smith.

   Riben liuxue sheng dou xuéxi
   Smith xiansheng jiao de yingyu yufa

5. He is not drinking the orange juice he ordered.

   Ta bu he ta yao de juzishui

6. We'll listen to the record* I bought at the Music Store [=Music Bookstore].

   women yao ting wo zai yingyue dian mai de luyin

7. He is writing a letter to the friend who invited him for dinner.

   Ta xie xin gei ta qing che wanfan de pengyou

8. He'll give some flowers (as presents) to his sister who works at the bank. It's her birthday today.

   Jintian shi ta de shengri
   Ta yao song yi shu huar gei zai yinghang gonzuo de tajiejie

9. Today, she is wearing the green skirt her mother bought for her.

   Jintian, ta chuan ta mama gei ta mai de lu qunzi

10. No one likes the movie that he recommended [=introduced] to us.

    Women dou bu xihuan tajieshao gei
    women de dianying

76

4/9/00

first part subject

Exercise XVI (Cont.)

B. 翻译 **Translation:** Apply the illustrated pattern to translate the sentences into Chinese.

Pattern #32b: Complex Sentence with Clause as Modifier: To give additional informarion on the subject.

    Note: This type of sentence may be viewed as combining two sentences of common subject.

Sub-sentence #1:	Subj. + Pred. 1	王老师喜欢喝酒.
Sub-sentence #2	Subj. + Pred. 2	王老师教我们汉语.

New Sentences:

Pred. 2 的 Subj. + Pred. 1   教我们汉语的王老师喜欢喝酒.

Pred. 1 的 Subj. + Pred. 2   喜欢喝酒的王老师教我们汉语.

1. The exchange students who live in our dormitory all study English and French.

   Zhu zai shushe de liuxuésheng dou xuéxi yingyu he fayu

2. None of the teachers who teach us grammar lives in the foreign language Institute.

   Zhu zai xuéyuan de laoshi dou bu jia women wai yu   zhu   yufa

3. That bunch of flowers he gave me are very beautiful.

   Ta gei wo de na shu haur hen piaoliang

4. All of the dancing parties given by the Chinese Department are boring.

   Zhong wen xi kai de wu hui dou mei you yisi

5. All of the foreign friends he introduced to me work in the bank.

   Ta gei wo jieshao de waigou pengyou dou zai yinhang gongzuo

6. The Japanese girls who come to the College to study are all very young.

   lai xué yuan xuéxi de riben gunian dou hen nianqing

7. The teacher who tutors us at night knows the address of the theatre.

   Wang shang fu dao women de laoshi zidao juchang de dizi

8. The classes I attended this afternoon are all very interesting.

   Wo canjia de xiawu de ke duo you yisi

9. (Our) classmates who live in Room 406 wish you a happy birthday.

   Zhu zai si ling liu fangjian hao de tongxue zhu ni gaoxing shengri.

10. Miss Zhang, who works at the movie theatre, tells me that she'll come to see you at 8:30 tonight.

   Zai dianyingyuan gongzuo de Zhang xiaojie gousi wo ta lai kan ni. ba dian ban wangshang

Exercise XVI (Cont.)

C. 词序 Word order: Rearrange the elements of each entry to make a grammatical sentence.

1. 你　　好　　生日　　祝

2. 学生　　年轻　　的　　那个　　中国人　　是

3. 花　　漂亮　　真　　束　　这

4. 她　　她妈妈　　象　　真

5. 他们　　跳舞　　不　　那儿　　在

6. 谁　　帕兰卡　　两　　电影　　票　　张　　送

7. 跳舞　　喜欢　　王太太　　不

8. 姑娘　　漂亮　　很　　都　　日本　　吗

9. 门　　请　　开

10. 他　　我们　　看看　　去　　吧

Exercise XVI (Cont.)

D. 用词 Choice of Words: Fill in the blanks with the most appropriate words, using one character for each blank.

1. 你好! _____ 进, _____ 坐, _____ 喝茶.

2. _____ 你生日好!

3. 这 _____ 花是我朋友 _____ (给) 我的.

4. "你想, 是红的花漂亮还是黄 _____ _____ _____ _____ ?"

   "红的花漂亮, 黄 _____ _____ _____ (*even more) _____ _____ ."

5. 她的生日 _____ 九月六 _____ . 你的生日 _____ _____ _____ _____ _____ ?

6. "你妹妹今年 _____ _____ (or _____ _____)?" "她今年十 _____ ."

7. 他们在哪儿 _____ 舞?

8. 朋友 _____ (给) 他很多生日 _____ * _____ * (gifts). 他很 _____ _____ .

9. "他是日本人吗?" "他不 _____ 日本人, 他 _____ 中国人 ."

10. 那个跳舞 _____ 姑娘 _____ 漂亮!

Exercise XVI (Cont.)

E. 问答 Answering Questions: Answer the following questions according to the actual situations about yourself or imagined situation.

1. 你今年多大？

2. 你的生日是哪一天？

3. 你是象你爸爸还是象你妈妈？

4. 你喜欢跳舞吗？

5. 谁常送你花？你常送谁花？

6. 星期天在花店买花的人很多吗？

7. 辅导你们汉语的老师是中国人吗？

8. 你爸爸买的衬衫都很漂亮吗？

9. 你大夫的那辆*车是不是日本车？

10. 他们都说书店的服务员很漂亮，你说呢？

Exercise XVII
(Lesson 22)

A. 翻译 Translation: Apply the illustrated pattern to translate the sentences into Chinese.

Pattern #33: **Ascriptive Sentence**: Using Verb-exist. 在/有 or Verb-id 是 to indicate location.

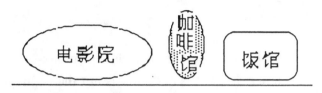

	(a)	**This place**	**is at / is on**	**this location / this side.**	
		NP-place	V-exist	NP-position	
[Examples]:		电影院	在	那儿.	
		饭馆	在	右*边儿.	
	(b)	**Place A**	**is on**	**place B's**	**this side.**
		NP-place	V-exist	NP-place+ (的)	NP-position
[Example]:		电影院	在	咖啡馆 (的)	左边.
	(c)	**(On) place A's**		**this side**	**is**	**place B.**
		(V-ex) NP-place (+的)		NP-location	V-id	NP-place
[Example]:		在咖啡馆的		左边	是	电影院.
	(d)	**(On) place A's**	**this side**	**there is/are**	**this/these place(s).**
		(V-ex) NP-place(+的) NP-loc.		V-exist	(#+M) NP-place
[Example]:		电影院	对面	有	两个书店,一个银行.

Pattern #34: **Word-/Phrase-of-location used as modifier**

	+	**of this side/location**	**'s**	**person / thing**	+
		NP-position +	的	NP	
[Examples]:		左边	的	人	是王老师.
他住在		里边	的	房间.	
		上边	的	两本杂志 很新.	

Note: In sentences of parallel clauses, the noun after 的 may be omitted if understood. Refer to Pattern #25 in Exercise (L. 16) and the following examples:

左边的椅子很新, 右*边的(椅子)也很新.
上边的词典是汉语词典, 下边的(词典)是英汉词典.

Exercise XVII (Cont.)

A. 翻译 Translation: (Cont.)

1. Shirley's home is behind the Foreign Language College. It has more than ten rooms.

Shirley de jia zai waiyu xuéyduan de houbian.
Tyou shi dou ge fanzi

2. The study is on the lower level (and) their bedrooms are on the upper level. [Note: Conjunction is not needed in the Chinese sentence and 和 is certainly is not the right word for it here. Do you know why?]

Shufang zai woshi de xiabian, woshi zai shufang de shangbian.

3. Her bedroom is to the left of her younger sister's bedroom and to the right of her parents' (bedroom). Her bedroom is in the middle*.

Ta de woshi zai Ta meimei de woshi de zoubian. Ta de woshi zai mama baba de woshi de youbian. Ta de woshi zai meimei de he mama baba de zhongjian

4. To the right of her sister's bedroom is the bathroom.

Xizaojian zai Ta jiejie de woshi de youbian

5. Across from her bedroom, there is another [*use 还有] bathroom and next to it is a small room where no one lives. Ta de woshi zai hua you xizaojian de duimian, xiaojian zai shao pangjian he zheii you ren zhu de pangbian. naiyou yige xizaojian zai ta de woshi de duimian, Pangbian you yige mei you ren zhu de yige xiao fangjian

6. The living room is next to the study and across from the dinning room.

Keting zai shufang de pangbian he canting de duimian

7. There are two big chairs and three smaller chairs in the living room.

liang ge ji he san ge xiao yizi zai keti a
keting you liang ge da yizi he san ge xiao yizi

8. The coffee table is between the two big chairs.

Kafei zhouzi zai liang ge da yizi de zhongjian

9. In the dinning room, there are many chairs and a dinning table.

duo ge yizi he yi ge can zhouzi zai keting

10. At the back of their house is a small garden. There are no flowers in the garden at this time.

Tamen de jia de houbian shi xiao huayuan, xianzai huayuan mei you hua.

Extra: Could you draw a picture illustrating Shirley's home based on the information provided in the preceding ten sentences?

Exercise XVII (Cont.)

shijiedity

A. 翻译 Translation: (Cont.)

11. The inner rooms are bedrooms and the outer room is a study.

Woshi zai fangzi de libian. Fangzi zai shufang de waibian

12. On the desk there are three books. The one on top is a grammar book; the one at the bottom is a world atlas; and the middle* one is the *Introduction to Chinese Folk Songs*.

Sozhuozi de shangbian shi san ge shu. Yi ge yufa shu zai shijie ditu zai zhongguo minge jieshao shu de shangbian shi jie ditu zai liang ge shu de xiabian. zhongyan minge jieshao shu zai liang ge shu de zhongjian

13. Across from the study are two bedrooms. The one on the left is her bedroom and the one on the right is her brother's.

liang ge woshi zai shufang de duimian. Ta de woshi zai ta didi de woshi de zoubian. Ta didi de woshi zai ta de woshi de youbian

14. There are chairs both inside and outside* the living room. The ones inside are new ones and the ones outside* are old ones.

yizi zai keting de libian he waibian. libian de yizi shi xin de. waibian de yizi shi jiu de.

15. There are banks on both sides [=两边(儿)] of our house: a small one on the left and a large one on the right.

Yi ge yinhang zai women de fangzi de liangbian. Xiao de zai women de fanzi de zoubian. da de zai fangzi de youbian

16. Winthrop's [*Can you make a Chinese name for Winthrop?] house has two gardens. The garden in the front does not have flowers, but the one in the back has many beautiful flowers.

Winthrop de fanzi you liang ge huayuan. Yi ge de zai fangzi de qianbian mei you huar. zai houbian de you dou haokan huar.

17. The building across (from here) is a bookstore. The house to the right is my friend's home.

zhe ge (building) zai shudian de duimian. zhe ge building zai wo pengyou de fangzi de youbian

18. Let's go to the restaurant across (the street) to eat.

women zou duimian qu restaurant chi

19. Are you going to the front reading room or the rear reading room?

Ni qu qianbian de yuelanshi haishi houbian de yuelanshi?

20. Is he in the study upstairs [=on the upper (level)] or in the study downstairs [=on the lower (level)]?

Ta zai shangbian de shufang haishi xiabian de shufang?

Exercise XVII (Cont.)

B. 词序 Word order: Rearrange the elements of each entry to make a grammatical sentence.

1. 厨房　　他们的　　大　　　　很

2. 有　　　花园　　一个　　　后边

3. 我　　　卧室　　的　　　　里边的房间　　　　是

4. 杂志　　图书馆　有　　　　里边　　　很多

5. 什么　　上边　～　是　　　　桌子

6. 电影　　的　　　怎么样　星期六

7. 茶　　　的　　　你的　　　是　　　吗　　　窗户*旁边

8. 中间*　在　　　洗澡间　两个卧室

9. 洗澡　　在　　　上边　　洗澡间　　的　　　他

10. 书房　　卧室　　后边　　　在

4/24/00

Exercise XVII (Cont.)

C. 用词 Choice of Words: Based on the illustration (which is supposed to be the diagram of your house), fill in the blanks with appropriate words, using one character for each blank.

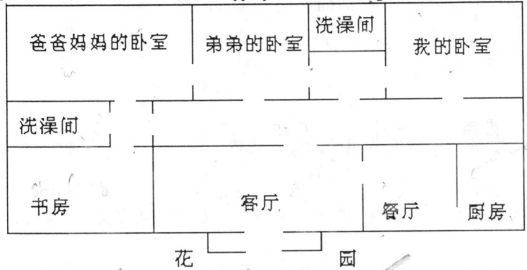

1. 我的卧室 _zai_ 餐厅 (的) _dui mian_ ✓

2. 爸爸妈妈的卧室 _zai_ 弟弟 (的) 卧室 (的) _zou bian_ ✓

3. 爸爸妈妈的卧室 (的) 旁边 _shi_ 一个 _xi zao jian_ ✓

4. 客厅 _zai_ 卧室 (的) _dui mian_ ✓

5. 客厅 (的) _zou_ 边 _shi_ 书房. ✓

6. 客厅 (的) _you_ *边 _shi_ 餐厅. ✓

7. 客厅 _zai_ 书房和餐厅 (的) _zhong jian_* ✓

8. 房子 (的) 前*边 _shi_ 一个花园, 后边 _mei you_ 花园. ✓

9. 厨房的 _zou_ 边 _shi_ 一个餐厅, 一个客厅, _ye shi_ 一个书房. ✓

10. 我们的房子 _you liang_ 个洗澡 _jian_, _san_ 个卧 _shi_. ✓

85

Exercise XVII (Cont.)

D. 问答 Answering Questions: Suppose someone you know just bought a new house. Tell us about this house by answering the following questions.

1. 他们的新房子怎么样？

2. 他们的新房子后边有没有花园？前边呢？花园里边有花吗？

3. 他们的房子有几个卧室？几个洗澡间？卧室旁边有没有洗澡间？

4. 他们的客厅大不大？客厅里边有几张桌子？几把*椅子？

5. 他的卧室在哪儿？

6. 他的书房在哪儿？在客厅对面吗？

7. 他总是在书房看书吗？

8. 桌子上边的书都是他的吗？椅子上边的呢？

9. 他常整理房间吗？谁帮他整理房间？

10. 谁帮他们整理花园？

Exercise XVIII
(Lesson 23)

A. 翻译 Translation: Apply the illustrated pattern to translate the sentences into Chinese.

Pattern #35: **Narrative Sentence**: Using (正)在+V-act ... (呢) to indicate action in progress.

	The subject	**is in the midst of**	**doing this**	**you know!**
	NP-person	(正)在	V-act (+Obj.)	(呢)
[Example]:	我们	正在	看电视	呢!

	The subject	**is right now**	**at this place**	**doing this**	**you know!**
	NP-person	(正)	在 + NP-pl	V-act (+Obj.)	呢
[Example]:	代表团	正	在工厂	访问.	

1. What are they doing now?   2. My mother is making a telephone call.

3. The delegation is paying a visit to the Chinese Department.

4. The delegate from the People's Daily* is interviewing [=访问] our English teacher.

5. His younger brother is playing outside.

6. They are looking at the pictures.

7. We are watching the television news.

8. The workers are cleaning up [=putting things in order] the garden.

9. The Friendship Delegation is visiting an automobile factory.

10. She is reviewing the text of lesson 22.

Exercise XVIII (Cont.)

B. 翻译 Translation: Apply the illustrated pattern to translate the sentences into Chinese.

Pattern #36: **Narrative Sentence**: Two actions with one in progress when the other takes place

	The time when A takes this action,			**B is in the midst of doing that.**
	NP1	V-act1	的时候	NP2	正/在/正在 V-act2
[Example]:	你	来	的时候, *sometime*	我们	正在吃饭. *eat rice*

时候 shí hou

shi you

Note: Following is an illustration of the comparative time-span of the two actions.

[Action#1]

[_____ Action #2 _____]

1. When he came, we were eating dinner.

Ta laide shi you, women zhengzai chi fan.

2. When you called, she was resting in her room.

Ni da dianhua de shi you, Ta zhengzai shui jiao zai ta de woshij

3. I was looking for you when you came.

Wo zhao ni de shi you, Ni zai lai de shi hou
zheng zai

4. She was waiting for you when you came to pick her up.

Ta dong ni shi you, ni zheng zai lai kai che ta de shi hou
zheng   jie

5. When I saw you, you were talking with the factory workers.

Wo kan ni de shi you, ni zhengzai tan gen gongchuan de
gong ren

6. When we went to the factory to visit, the workers were singing.

women qu canguan gongchang de shihou, gong ren zhengzai chang ger

7. At the time when you get married, I will be visiting China.

nimen jiehun de shi you, wǒ zhengzai canguan Zhongguo

8. When you entered the kitchen, we were helping mother cook.

nijin chufang de shi hou, women zhengzai bangzhu mama zuo fan

9. When you called, I was just thinking of calling you.

ni da dianhua de shi you, Wo zhengzai xiang gei ni da.

10. When you were writing to her, she must also be thinking about you.

Ni xie ta de shi you, Ta ye xiang ni,
xin gei

yi ding zheng zai

88

Exercise XVIII (Cont.)

C. 词序 Word order: Rearrange the elements of each entry to make a grammatical sentence.

1. 他   休息   正在   吗

2. 正在   他们   报   看

3. 接   客厅   电话   正在   她

4. 中国   代表团   在   访问

5. 复习   呢   我   课文   在

6. 都   看   我们   电视   正在   呢

7. 正在   她   你   等   家里

8. 后边   她妹妹   在   玩儿   房子

9. 正在   写信   我   他   来   的时候

10. 城里   代表团   在   工厂   一个   参观

Exercise XVIII (Cont.)

D. 用词 Choice of Words: Fill in the blanks with the most appropriate words, using one character for each blank.

1. 他们 _____ 不 _____ 家里吗？

2. 孩子们 _____ _____ 花园里玩儿．

3. 你去接他的 _____ _____ 他 _____ 在 _____ 电话．

4. 你来 _____ _____ _____ , 我们 _____ 看电视新闻 _____ ．

5. 代表团 _____ _____ 中国 _____ _____ ．

6. "喂！我 _____ 小丁, 请她 _____ 电话." "好！请等 _____ _____ ."

7. 报上 _____ 他们的照片 _____ _____ ？

8. 他们去看你 _____ _____ _____ , 你在 _____ 什么？

9. 谁 _____ _____ 听音乐？ (*who is listening to music at this time?)

10. 那个留学生 _____ _____ 城 _____ 边 _____ _____ 一个工厂．

Exercise XVIII (Cont.)

E. 问答 Answering Questions: Answer the following questions according to your real-life situation.

1. 你在作什么？

2. 谁在看报？他在哪儿看报？

3. 你爸爸妈妈在哪儿吃饭？

4. 你上课的时候，你的好朋友正在作什么？

5. 你复习课文的时候，有没有人在看电视？

6. 你休息的时候，你的室友 (roommate) 在作什么呢？

7. 你去看你朋友他的时候，谁在他家？

8. 明天你有空吗？

9. 我们去参观咖啡工厂，好吗？

10. 我们怎么去呢？开车去吗？

Exercise XIX
(Lesson 24)

A. 翻译 Translation: Apply **all three** illustrated patterns to translate **each** of the sentences into Chinese.

Pattern #37: Interrogative Sentence Verifying a Statement

(a)	<u>Statement</u>	,	是吗?
[Example]:	她上课的时候很认真		是吗?
(b)	<u>Statement</u>	,	是不是?
[Example]:	你们每天上午锻炼		是不是?
(c)	<u>Subj.</u> 是不是	<u>Predicate</u>	?
[Examples]:	她 是不是	上课的时候很认真?	
	她上课的时候 是不是	很认真?	
	你们 是不是	每天上午锻炼?	

Note: (1) In pattern #37(c), the "...的时候" phrase may be grouped with the subject or the predicate as illustrated by the first and second sentences. The point of interrogation is, however, on what follows the expression "是不是." (2) Also review Patterns #2 and #15.

1. He likes to eat the dimsum his mother made, doesn't he?

2. Do you often practice Chinese together?

3. They are going to take a train to go to the rural area, aren't they?

4. Are they all enthusiastic when they do their physical training?

5. The new words that the teacher taught today are all very difficult, aren't they?

Exercise XIX (Cont.)

B. 词序 Word order: Rearrange the elements of each entry to make a grammatical sentence.

1. 来　　我家　　你　　玩　　请

2. 古波　去　　火车　　农村　　坐　　他爸爸　看

3. 去　　他们　　锻炼　　哪儿

4. 点心　谁　　作　　是　　那些　　的

5. 老师　常常　　很难的　我　　问　　问题

6. 吃　　他妈妈　点心　　他　　给　　作　　常

7. 书　　那些　　不是　　买　　的　　我

8. 他　　正在　　打电话　我　　给我　　的时候　锻炼

9. 他　　这些　　京剧票　是　　都　　买　　的

10. 很　　学习　　总是　　的时候　她　　认真

Exercise XIX (Cont.)

C. 用词 Choice of Words: Fill in the blanks with the most appropriate words, using one character for each blank.

1. 她的家 _____ 城里,不 _____ 农 _____.

2. 她常常 _____ 火车 _____ 这儿玩儿.

3. 明天我 _____ 飞机 (fei1ji1, airplane)_____ 欧洲 (Europe*) _____ 朋友.

4. 这是我姐姐 _____ 你们作_____ 点心.

5. 他现在很 _____ : 每天上午锻 _____ , 下午工作, 晚上 _____
    学习汉语.

6. 我爸爸妈妈回家的 _____ _____ , 我 _____ 在 _____ 练习.

7. 我们 _____ 工厂 _____ _____ (*visit) 的时候, 工人都_____ 休息.

8. 今天上课 _____ 时候, 老师 _____ _____ 我两 _____ 问题.

9. 今天老师_____ 的课文_____ 语法我_____ 不懂. 我没(有)* (*did not)
    _____ _____ 老师 _____ _____ 问题.

10. 他是一个很 _____ _____ 的学生. 他学习 _____ 时候很 _____ _____ ,
    锻炼 _____ _____ _____ 也很 _____ _____ .

Exercise XIX (Cont.)

D. 问答 Answering Questions: Answer the following questions according to the actual situations about yourself and your own opinion.

1. 你的爸爸妈妈是农民吗？

2. 谁的爸爸妈妈是农民？

3. 你每天都作语法练习吗？

4. 你每天都锻炼吗？你什么时候锻炼？

5. 你知道不知道你吃的饭是谁作的？是给谁作的？

6. 学汉语难不难？写汉字呢？

7. 你朋友常来宿舍看你，是吗？

8. 谁常去农村？他去那儿作什么？

9. 今天老师教的课文你懂不懂？

10. 你不懂的时候，你是不是问老师？

Exercise XX
(Review: L. 19-24)

A. 用词 Choice of Words: Fill in the blanks with the most appropriate words, using one character for each blank. Note that the entries together form a story.

1. 小王说他女朋友明天 _____ 城外边 _____ 火车 _____ 看他.

2. 我 _____ 小王她 _____ 上午来 _____ _____ 下午来.

3. 小王 _____ 他上午九 _____ _____ 去 _____ 她.

4. 我不知道她来以后, _____ 住在小王(_____)姐姐家 _____ _____ 住在学生宿舍.

5. 我 _____ 小王他女朋友 _____ _____ _____ 住在宿舍.
   他说不一定(*).

6. 我问小王 _____ _____ _____ 很想他女朋友.

7. 他说他想她, 他 _____ 想吃她作 _____ 点心.

8. 我问小王: "你们在一起 _____ _____ _____ , 她常 _____ 你作点心 _____ , _____ _____ ?"

9. 小王说: "我们 _____ 一起 _____ _____ _____ , 她常 _____ 点心 _____ 我 _____ , 我 _____ 常 _____ 点心 _____ 她 _____ ."

10. 小王 _____ 女朋友来的 _____ _____ , 我 _____ _____ 卧室 _____ _____
    看报. 小王 _____ 我们介绍. 认识小王的女朋友我很 _____ _____ .

Exercise XX (Cont.)

B. 作文 Composition:

1. Write a passage about the things 谢文美 will do in August. During that month, her parents will be returning from their visit to Japan and the daughter of her parents' Japanese friend will come home with 文美's parents to study in the English department of her college. Later that month her younger brother will celebrate his birthday.

2. Write a passage about a telephone call you made to your sister/brother/friend. The two of you talked about the movie he/she saw recently, which you had recommended to him/her earlier. You also told him/her what you had been doing recently.

Exercise XX (Cont.)

C. 作文 Composition: Write a passage describing the following map.

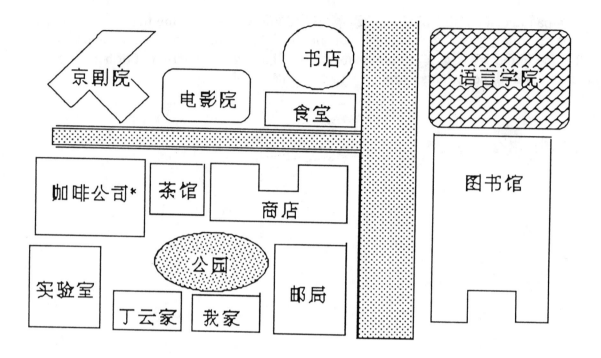

Exercise XX (Cont.)

D. 作文 Composition: Write a passage describing the following picture of 王三's bedroom.

Exercise XXI
(Lesson 25)

A. 翻译 Translation: Apply the illustrated pattern to translate the sentences into Chinese.

Pattern #38: Narrative Sentence with Modifier Describing Manner of Action

	Someone	**acts**	**in**	**this manner.**
	NP	V-act	manner marker 得	Modifier-state
[Example]:	我	写	得	很慢.

Note: No object of the verb is used in this pattern.

1. He sings well.

2. Ding Yun swims fast. [The word "游泳" may be analyzed as a Verb-Object combination.]

3. She studies diligently [=earnestly].

4. They have had a good time [=they played happily.]

5. They all came quickly.

6. We did not sleep well at night. [睡觉 may also be viewed as a Verb-Object combination.]

7. You worry [=think] too much.

8. She drives too fast.

9. Mr. Zhang teaches conscientiously.

10. You speak (Chinese) fluently*.

Exercise XXI (Cont.)

B. 翻译 Translation: Apply the illustrated pattern to translate the sentence into Chinese.

Pattern #39: Narrative Sentence with Modifier Describing Manner of Action -- Part 2

Someone	**in doing this**	**does (it)**	**in**	**this manner.**
Subj.	Topic	Action	M-Marker	M-Modifier
NP	V-act + Obj.	V-act	得	Adv.
[Example]: 我	写字	写	得	很慢.

Note: (1) This pattern includes a topic which in structure is a verb-object combination and in function is similar to a gerund in English. Since the topic is about the action, it includes the same verb as that for the action. (2) The positions of the subject and the topic may be switched. When the topic precedes the subject, the first verb may be omitted. Also, when the topic precedes the subject, the sentence may be called a "topical sentence." In a "topical sentence," the topic(s) is/are the focus of the sentence; a typical example is one involving listing, comparison or contrast such as the following:

(写)字, 我写得很慢, (说)话, 我说得很快.

1. She swims fast but her younger brother swims very slow.

2. We don't cook very well. She does?

3. As for teaching swimming, my coach does [=teaches] pretty well.

4. I ate too much fish.

5. They all speak Chinese clearly*.

6. He did not park correctly.

7. Those two young ladies drank too much soup.

8. Do you sleep very late?

9. She always prepares her lessons [use "text"] enthusiastically.

10. He dances beautifully but writes badly.

Exercise XXI (Cont.)

C. 词序 **Word order:** Rearrange the elements of each entry to make a grammatical sentence.

1. 她   很快   游泳   得   游

2. 你们   得   饭   作   作   很不错

3. 认真   锻炼   很   我们   都   得

4. 今天   喝酒   喝   得   太多   你

5. 他   好不好   字   写   得   写

6. 请   停车   前边   工厂   在

7. 吧   吃   面包   再   一点儿

8. 爸爸   她(的)   (一)位   教练   是   游泳

9. 宿舍   河里   游泳   后边   在   他们   的

10. 他   我   请   喝   常   去他家   茶

Exercise XXI (Cont.)

D. 用词 Choice of Words: Fill in the blanks with the most appropriate words, using one character for each blank.

1. 你吃 _____ 很少. _____ 吃点儿_____ !

2. 他说 _____ 太快. 我听不 _____ _____ (clearly)*.

3. 他开车 _____ _____ 太快. 我不要他来 _____ 我. 我走去*.

4. 谢老师教汉语 _____ _____ 很 _____ _____ .

5. 他停车 _____ _____ 哪儿了？

6. 他妈妈常 _____ 鱼汤_____ 他 _____ .

7. 那 _____ 河的旁边 _____ (一)个工厂.

8. 王兰是我的_____ _____ . 她教我游_____ .

9. 他 (_____) 点心_____ 得不错, 我很喜欢_____ .

10. 你 _____ 字 _____ _____ 真好!

Exercise XXI (Cont.)

E. 问答 Answering Questions: Answer the following questions according to the actual situations about yourself.

1. 你作饭作得好还是你爸爸作饭作得好？

2. 你写字总是写得很快吗？

3. 你和你家人(your family)去玩儿的时候, 谁开车？谁准备吃的？

4. 谁开车开得好？谁作饭作得好？

5. 你妈妈是你的游泳教练, 是吗？

6. 你晚上休息得好不好？

7. 今天教的课文, 你复习得怎么样了？

8. 你们教授教书*教得怎么样？

9. 你喜欢钓鱼吗？你常常去钓鱼, 是不是？

10. 我吃奶酪吃得很少, 你呢？

Exercise XXII
(Lesson 26)

A. 翻译 Translation: Apply the illustrated pattern to translate the sentences into Chinese.

Pattern #40: Narrative Sentence: Using potential markers 能/可以/想/要/会 to indicate possibility.

	Someone		may potentially	take this action.
	NP	<neg.>	Potential Markers	VP
			能/可以/想/要/会	V-act + Obj.
[Examples]:	我		想	去日本.
	我不知道什么时候		能 / 可以	去.
	我去的时候		要	跟古兰一起去.
	她		会	说日语.

Note: The five potential-markers indicate different types of possibilities: 能 may indicate a general potential or a physical ability. 可以 implies permission, allowance, or agreement. 想 indicates a mental inclination while 要 presents a decision. 会 is a little different from the others; it may refer to a learned capability, a definite possibility or a strong prediction.

1. His mother wants him to be a doctor, but he doesn't want to be a doctor.

2. I don't know how to speak Japanese.　　　3. We are thinking of going to see a movie.

4. "Neither of us knows how to swim. Will you teach us?" "Sure [=no problem], I'll teach you."

5. His brother really knows how to cook.　　　　6. Could you phone Professor Ding?

7. You are not allowed to fish in this river but you may fish in the river beside it.

8. "I would like to invite you over for dinner. Could you come?" "I'll certainly be there [=come]."

9. In that college, students are not allowed to eat in the Professors' Dinning Hall.

10. I don't know how to drive. I want to learn. Will you teach me?

Exercise XXII (Cont.)

B. 词序 Word order: Rearrange the elements of each entry to make a grammatical sentence.

1. 想   民歌   学习   你   哪国的

2. 理想   当   我的   老师   是

3. 去   想   游泳   他   不

4. 你   作家   研究   要   呢   哪位

5. 了解   我   中国   农村   问题   的   不

6. 当   当   你   不错   得   翻译

7. 研究   俩   他们   要   都   京剧

8. 那   有名   小说   很   本

9. 我   今天   明天   想去   或者   北京   就

10. 不   容易   翻译   很   当   啊

Exercise XXII (Cont.)

C. 用词 Choice of Words: Fill in the blanks with the most appropriate words, using one character for each blank.

1. 我以后想 _____ (to be a) 老师, 他 _____ _____ 大夫.

2. 我们再谈 _____ 吧! 互相了解 _____ _____ .

3. 鲁迅是一 _____ 有名的 _____ _____ .

4. 我们 _____ 想明年一月 _____ 去中国学习.

5. 翻译 _____ _____ 能 _____ _____ 两国人民的了解.

6. 以后我 _____ 学习法语 _____ _____ 日语.

7. 学生都 _____ _____ 认真学习.

8. 你以后想 _____ 什么工作? 我想你 _____ _____ 当作家.

9. 那个医院有很多 _____ 名 _____ 大夫.

10. 研究中国文学不太难, _____ 不太 _____ _____ .

Exercise XXII (Cont.)

D. 问答 Answering Questions: Answer the following questions according to the actual situations about yourself.

1. 今天晚上你想作什么？

2. 以后你想作什么？你想当翻译吗？你会说法语或者德语吗？

3. 你想是当翻译有意思还是当教练有意思？

4. 谈话能加深朋友的了解吗？

5. 你会不会游泳？大学后边儿的河里可以不可以游泳？

6. 河旁边能不能停车？

7. 从德国来的留学生回国以后作什么？

8. 你想去哪儿参观？你会开车吗？

9. 你想，找一个理想的工作容易吗？

10. 你说，到中国去当翻译，好不好？

Exercise XXIII
(Lesson 27)

A. 翻译 **Translation**: Apply the illustrated pattern to translate the sentences into Chinese.

Pattern #41: **Narrative Sentence**: Using 了 (without quantitative measure) to indicate that an action has been initiated or (with quantitative measure) that an action has been initiated and reached a certain extent.

	(a)	**The subj,**	**has taken an action**	**and reached this level**	**on this.**
		NP	V-act + IM 了	Number + Measure	Obj.-NP
[Examples]:		张小姐	来 了		
		我们	喝 了		汤.
		他	买 了	两本	书.

	(b)	**About this,**	**someone has taken an action**	**and reached this extent.**
		Topic: NP	Subj.: NP + V-act + IM 了	Quantity: <#> <M>
[Example]:		葡萄酒	我们 喝 了	一瓶.

Note: For more on "**Topical Sentence**," review notes on Pattern #39, Exercise XXI ((L. 25)

1. The movie has started.

2. We caught six fish.

3. I drank some grape wine and I also tasted a little Maotai.

4. At dinner [When I was eating dinner), I drank two cups of tea.

5. I bought some ham and cheese.

6. He answered the teacher's questions.

7. When I was in China, I became acquainted with two famous writers.

8. I have practiced the characters and I have also prepared the text.

9. The Chinese ambassador gave a reception.

10. I attended the embassy's cocktail party.

Exercise XXIII (Cont.)

B. 翻译 Translation: Apply the illustrated patterns to translate the sentences into Chinese.

Pattern #42: **Narrative Sentence**: Using 没(有) to indicate that an action has not been initiated.

(a)	**The subject**	**has not**	**taken an action**	**on this.**
	NP	Non-IM 没(有)	V-act	Obj.-NP
[Examples]:	王参赞	没有	参加	招待会.
	我	没	问.	

(b)	**To this,**	**the subject**	**has not taken**	**this action.**
	Topic:NP	Subj.-NP	Non-IM 没(有)	V-act
[Example]:	茅台酒	她	没	尝.

1. He did not translate those three words.

2. The attendant did not help us.

3. None of the members [=people] of the delegation came to the welcome party.

4. The coach did not teach us swimming.

5. She did not wear that red shirt I gave to her.

6. The Ambassador came but not his wife.

7. I ate some Chinese food [=dishes] but I did not use chopsticks.

8. He provided [=prepared] wine but he did not provide any mineral water.

9. We all tasted the Maotai but he did not.

10. He did not cook the rice and he did not cook any dishes. What do we eat?

Exercise XXIII (Cont.)

C. 翻译 Translation: Apply the illustrated patterns to translate the sentences into Chinese.

Pattern #43: **Interrogative Sentence:** Using <V-act 了 ... 没有 > structure to inquire if an action has taken place.

	(a)	**The subject**	**has taken this action**		**or has not?**
		Subj.: NP	V-act +	IM 了	Non-IM 没有
[Example]:		大使夫人	来	了	没有?
	(b)	**The subject**	**has taken an action on this**		**or hasn't?**
		Subj.:NP	V-act IM 了 +	Obj.	Non-IM 没有
[Example]:		你们	学习了 中国文化		没有?
	(c)	**On this,**	**the subject**	**has taken an action**	**or not?**
		Topic: NP	NP	V-act + IM 了	Non-IM 没有
[Example]:		中国文化	你们	学习 了	没有?

Note: This pattern is similar to the "<+> <->" type of interrogative structure introduced by Patterns #15 and #17 in Exercises VII and VIII (L. 13 & 14). Other types of interrogative sentences, such as "Statement + 吗," "the tag-question with 呢," etc.. may also be applied to narrative sentences the same way as they are applied to other types of sentences.

1. Has the movie started yet?

2. Did you buy any grapes?

3. Do you have any chopsticks?

4. Have you made the telephone call?

5. Did you try on that shirt?

6. Has the reception party started?

7. Did you invite the culture counselor and his wife?

8. Have you tasted that French brandy*?

9. Is everyone here yet? [Has everyone come?]

10. Has Madame Wang introduced you (plural) to each other?

Exercise XXIII (Cont.)

D. 词序 Word order: Rearrange the elements of each entry to make a grammatical sentence.

1. 开始　　还　　　　招待会　　没有

2. 酒　　　喝　　　　他　　　了　　　　两杯

3. 请进　　都　　　　你们　　来了

4. 不　　　用筷子　　会　　　太　　　　我

5. 高兴　　我　　　　认识　　能　　　　你们　　　非常

6. 参加　　大使馆　　大家　　酒会　　　到　　　　请

7. 干杯　　人民　　　两国　　为　　　　的　　　　友谊

8. 筷子　　留学生　　两位　　会　　　　都　　　　这　　　用

9. 菜　　　作　　　　作　　　好　　　　很　　　　他　　　得

10. 尝尝　　菜　　　　我弟弟　　的　　　　作　　　请

Exercise XXIII (Cont.)

E. 用词 Choice of Words: Fill in the blanks with the most appropriate words, using one character for each blank.

1. 下午我们去饭馆 _____ _____. 我们要 _____ 三 _____ 菜, 一 _____ 汤, 我们没 _____ 酒.

2. 他 _____ 中国菜 _____ _____ 很好.

3. _____ 大家的健康 _____ 杯

4. 我上午 _____ 他 _____ 电话, 他不 _____ 家. 我想现在 _____ _____ _____ _____ (...give it another try).

5. 筷子我会 _____ 了, 中国菜我 _____ 不会 _____.

6. 我去大使馆 _____ _____ 了一 _____ 招待会, 喝 _____ 两 _____ 茅台 _____. 还看 _____ 一 _____ 中国电影.

7. 能 _____ _____ 你的生日舞会, 我非常 _____ _____.

8. 我买 ___ 一 ___ 一九三六年 ___ 法国葡萄酒, 请大家 ___ ___.

9. 他今天作了很多事: 上午 _____ _____ 练习, 下午 _____ _____ _____ 房间, 晚上 _____ 作 _____ 饭. 可是他 _____ 写信.

10. 这是中文 _____ 的教授王 _____ _____ 和 (他) _____ _____. _____ 教授 _____ 我们中国文学, _____ 夫人 _____ 大使馆 工作.

Exercise XXIII (Cont.)

F. 问答 Answering Questions: Answer the following questions based on the assumption that there a welcome party for the exchange students took place last week.

1. 欢迎留学生的招待会,谁去参加了?

2. 大家都去了吗?

3. 招待会有什么酒?

4. 你可以不可以喝酒? 你会不会喝酒? 你喜欢喝酒吗? 你喝了酒吗?

5. 参加招待会的人都会用筷子吗?

6. 中国大使馆的文化参赞来了吗? 你认识不认识他?

7. 你朋友问你:"那个鱼汤是我作的. 你尝了没有?" 你怎么回答?

8. 课文你复习了没有? 生字都认识了吗?

9. 招待会以后你们去看了电影吗? 请了老师没有?

10. 招待会以前谁去了大使馆? 他去作什么?

Exercise XXIV
(Lesson 28)

A. 翻译 **Translation**: Apply the illustrated pattern to translate the sentences into Chinese.

Pattern #44: **Narrative Sentence**: Using Initiation-Marker 了 to report on the occurrence of an event, or a new situation.

	(a)	**This event**	**has taken place.**
		Sentence	IM 了
[Example]:		我给我爸爸妈妈写信	了.

[Changed from a previous situation: 我(还)没给我爸爸妈妈写信.]

	(b)	**The subject**	**is no longer in this state.**
		Subj.: NP	(Neg.) V-state/exist, etc. 了
[Example]:		代表团	不在工厂了.

[Change from a previous situation: 代表团在工厂.]

Note: (1) A 了 ("le") attached to the end of a sentence indicates that the event described in the sentence is supposedly a new situation to the listener. If it is attached to a positive statement, the sentence reports an event which has just taken place. If it is attached to a negative statement, the sentence means that the subject is no longer in the state described by the predicate. In either case, the sentence reports a new situation. Thus, in the example for Pattern #44 (a), the projected listener understood that prior to the statements, the subject had not yet written the letter. The statement is reporting a new situation: the subject has now written the letter. Similarly, in the example for (b), the subject's not being in the factory is a new situation. In other words, before the statement (b) was made, the projected listener's understanding was that the delegation was in the factory. Example for (b) informs the listener that the delegation has left and is no longer in the factory.
(2) While in this type of sentence the entire event is considered as a whole, in a sentence with "le" immediately following a verb of action the emphasis is on the action and the word "le" indicates the initiation of that action. It should be noted that "le" is not a "past-tense suffix." While the two types of sentences introduced in the previous lesson and this lesson may sometimes be translated into the same English sentence, each has a different emphasis.

1. The delegation has (now) come.

2. Guess what? [=Do you know?]   (Contrary to what you might have expected,) we went to see the football game!

3. When I lived at home, I did not like to eat cheese, but after I started living in the dormitory, I have come to like to eat cheese.

Exercise XXIV (Cont.)

A. 翻译 Translation: (Cont.)

4. He is finally cleaning up his room.

5. "I bought a Chinese dictionary." "Really! You [finally] bought a dictionary!"

6. She is not our coach any more. She is now a volleyball*-game referee.

7. He has finally called us (on the telephone).   8. [Trust me!] I did give him the hat.

9. I have gone to the embassy to get the visa.   10. We may now go to the skating rink [=field].

11. The Chinese Department team has had a ping-pong* match with the Exchange Student team.

12. The Chinese Department team won [for a change!] .

13. My brother's friend has come. My brother is no longer angry.

14. They have gone to visit the shoe factory.   15. We don't have any question anymore.

16. He is no longer doing research on French literature; he is researching Chinese music now.

17. It is winter now. Those little children are not playing outside anymore.

18. Her younger sister has (now) learned to [=know how to] kick the ball.

19. She ate breakfast today [for the first time!].   20. The referee has finally come.

Exercise XXIV (Cont.)

B. 翻译 Translation: Apply the illustrated pattern to translate the sentences into Chinese.

Pattern #45: **Interrogative Sentence**: Asking if the action has taken place-- Part 2

The subject	has or has not taken this action			to this object?
NP	V-act	没	V-act	NP
[Examples]: 他们	买	没	买	京剧票?
他	整	没	整理	房间?

Note: This is an abbreviated form of Pattern #43. It is a general practice to use only the first character of the v-act word before 没.

1. Did he go to the embassy?

2. Did he participate in the football game?

3. Did the delegation visit the maotai factory?

4. Did you do (your) homework [=exercise]?

5. Did they go skating?

6. Has the movie started yet?

7. Did she answer the ambassador's questions?

8. Did they entertain [=招待] the counselor's wife?

9. Have you packed [=put the luggage in order] yet?

10. Did you all do (your) physical training?

Exercise XXIV (Cont.)

C. 翻译 **Translation**: Apply the illustrated pattern to translate the sentences into Chinese.

Pattern #46: Interrogative Sentence: Asking if a new situation has taken pace.

	This new situation	**has taken place**	**has (it) not?**
	Sub.: NP + V-act + Obj.: NP	IM-了	Non-IM 没有?
[Example]:	你去办签证	了	没有?

1. Have you had [=eaten] lunch yet?

2. Has the coach of the university team come yet?

3. Did he (finally) take care of the visa-application?

4. Did you watch the ball game last night (after all)?

5. Have you packed your suitcase?

6. Have you bought the skates?

7. Have you gone skating this winter?

8. Has her sister cooked breakfast yet?

9. Have all the referees left yet?

10. Has the football game started yet?

Exercise XXIV (Cont.)

D. 翻译 Translation: Apply the illustrated pattern to translate the sentences into Chinese.

Pattern #47: **Narrative Sentence of Sequential Actions**

	Subj. A	**after completing act. 1**	**Subj. (A /) B**	**then**	**takes act. 2**
	Subj.: NP	V-act1 了 + Obj.	NP	就	V-act2 + Obj.
[Examples]:	我	打了电话		就	去大使馆.
	他	买了书	我们	就	走.

1. Having entered the room, they drink some tea.

2. Having bought the tickets, they entered the theatre.

3. After I arrive in China, I'll go see the Great Wall.

4. After he packs, he'll leave.

5. After the ambassador gets here [=has come], the reception will starts.

6. After watching the ball game, they all returned home.

7. When(ever) they lose, his father will say that the coach is not good.

8. After you buy the skates, we can go skating.

9. You should pack right after you buy the suitcase.

10. After getting into the city, I'll go visit (our teacher) Mr. Zhang.

Exercise XXIV (Cont.)

E. 词序 Word order: Rearrange the elements of each entry to make a grammatical sentence.

1. 他　　　签证　　　办　　　　大使馆　　　去

2. 跟　　　工厂队　　农村队　　足球　　　比赛

3. 帽子　　冰鞋　　　两双　　　一顶　　　我想买　　跟

4. 午饭　　就　　　　吃了　　　吧　　　　出发

5. 球队　　的　　　　他们　　　赢了　　　比　　　六　　　九

6. 裁判　　总是　　　说　　　　公平　　　不　　　别

7. 我们　　电影　　　票　　　　了　　　　看　　　买　　　就去

8. 来　　　比赛　　　裁判　　　了　　　　开始　　　就

9. 谈　　　问题　　　你们　　　这个　　　没谈

10. 面包　　尝了　　　你　　　　没有　　　奶酪

Exercise XXIV (Cont.)

F. 用词 Choice of Words: Fill in the blanks with the most appropriate words, using one character for each blank.

1. 昨天的球 _____ 大学 _____ 赢了, 二十 _____ 七.

2. 你复习 _____ 课文 _____ 去休息吧.

3. 你们队输 _____ 你 _____ 说 _____ _____ 不公平.

4. 他下 _____ 课 _____ 去踢 _____.

5. 我 _____ 了代表团 _____ 去 _____ _____ 招待会.

6. 我 _____ 了球赛 _____ 去 _____ 签证.

7. 明天他要 _____ 大使夫人一起到 _____ _____ 场*去 _____ 网球*.

8. 我 _____ 去公园*滑冰,可是我没有 _____ 鞋,我不能去 _____.

9. "你没有冰鞋? 没问题! 我 _____ 你一 _____ 吧!" "非常 _____ _____."

10. 昨天的篮球* _____ ,我们队赢了,我真 _____ _____."

Exercise XXIV (Cont.)

G. 问答 Answering Questions: Answer the following questions according to the actual situations about yourself or imagined situations.

1. 你们昨天去城里玩得怎么样？

2. 你喜欢打乒乓球还是喜欢踢足球？

3. 你买了冰鞋我们就去滑冰，好不好？

4. 昨天的篮球*友谊赛哪队赢了？几比几？

5. 你们什么时候去吃午饭？ [Use "… 了 … 就 …"]

6. 你的箱子整理得怎么样了？

7. 昨天晚上你看电视了没有？

8. 电视上的球赛怎么样？教练怎么样？裁判呢？

9. 你今天吃了早饭作了什么？

10. 你办了签证就去日本吗？

Exercise XXV
(Lesson 29)

A. 翻译 Translation: Apply the illustrated pattern to translate the sentences into Chinese.

Pattern #48: Narrative Sentence: Predicting a new situation that will soon take place

	The Subj.	**will soon**	**take this action.**	
	NP	要/快要/就快要/就要	V-act	了
[Examples]:	我们	就要	去滑冰	了.
	飞机	快要	到	了.
	足球赛	就快要	开始	了.

Note: there is a slight difference among these four expressions in terms of degree of immediacy. The immediacy increases from 要 to 快要 to 就快要 to 就要.

1. We are going to a class soon.

2. Spring will soon be here [=come].

3. They are going to China soon.

4. I will soon pack my luggage.

5. We will soon use a new book.

6. We will soon go to the Embassy to get our visa.

7. The airplane will soon take off.

8. My classmates will come soon.

9. He'll be back soon. I am so happy!

10. The airplane will soon arrive in Beijing.

Exercise XXV (Cont.)

B. 翻译 Translation: Apply the illustrated pattern to translate the sentences into Chinese.

Pattern #49: **Narrative Sentence**: Predicting a new situation to take place in the near future-- with specific time indicated.

	The subj.	will at this time		take this action.
	NP	Time + 就 / 就要		V-act + 了
[Examples]:	王老师	明天	就要	离开 了.
	(中学)	一月三号	就	开始上课 了.
	飞机	两点钟	就	起飞 了.

Note: Since a specific time is indicated, the general time expressions 快要 and 就快要 become inappropriate in this pattern.

1. The airplane will take off as early as 5:30 p.m.

2. They will go to China as early as next summer.

3. He'll pick you up at 2:30 p.m.

4. We will leave our parents as early as this fall.

5. We will start using the new Chinese book next January.

6. I will write to my teacher this evening.

7. We'll arrive at the airport at 1:15.

8. Professor Wang will teach us Chinese folk songs this afternoon.

9. I'll go learn to drive tomorrow morning.

10. Classes will be over at 11:30.

Exercise XXV (Cont.)

C. 词序 Word order: Rearrange the elements of each entry to make a grammatical sentence.

1. 明年　　中国　　去　　看　　我们　　他们

2. 平安　　你们　　一路　　祝

3. 开　　了　　火车　　要　　快　　就

4. 去　　三点钟　　接你　　机场　　一定　　我

5. 大家　　紧　　站(得)　　一点　　请

6. 身体　　注意　　要　　也要　　学习　　努力

7. 就要　　离开　　了　　所以　　他们　　很难过　　我

8. 健康　　你们　　祝　　身体

9. 就　　你们　　吧　　休息　　整理整理

10. 可是　　就要　　了　　好朋友　　他们　　是　　分开

Exercise XXV (Cont.)

D. 用词 Choice of Words: Fill in the blanks with the most appropriate words, using one character for each blank.

1. 他 ＿＿ 去机场＿＿ 朋友,＿＿ ＿＿ 不能来 ＿＿ ＿＿ 舞会.

2. 他妈妈＿＿ 他 ＿＿ ＿＿ 身体.

3. 明年秋 ＿＿ 我 ＿＿ 要去中国＿＿.

4. 请 ＿＿ 我们＿＿ 一张相.

5. 他知道他 ＿＿ ＿＿ 离开了,＿＿ ＿＿ 他不愿 ＿＿ 离开.

6. 飞机就要 ＿＿ ＿＿ 了,请大家＿＿ 飞机吧

7. 别忘 ＿＿,到＿＿ 北京＿＿ 给我 ＿＿ 信.

8. "我们非常感谢您." "＿＿ ＿＿,这是我 ＿＿ ＿＿ 作的."

9. ＿＿ 难过! 我们很快 ＿＿ ＿＿ 见面了.

10. 李老师 ＿＿ 书很认真,＿＿ ＿＿ 学生学习得都很＿＿ ＿＿.

Exercise XXV (Cont.)

E. 问答 **Answering Questions:** Answer the following questions assuming that you are about to take a trip to China.

1. 你去中国是夏天去还是秋天去？

2. 你要坐飞机去还是坐船*去？

3. 你是不是要坐飞机去？

4. 飞机几点起飞？

5. 从你家去机场怎么去？坐火车去吗？

6. 你爸爸妈妈去送你吗？他们身体怎么样？

7. 在机场谁要给你们照相？

8. 就要离开家了，你难过吗？

9. 你高兴吗？为什么 (for what, why)？

10. 你去中国以后要作什么？

Exercise XXVI
(Lesson 30)

A. 翻译 Translation: Apply the illustrated pattern to translate the sentences into Chinese.

Pattern #50: **Descriptive Statement on Geographical Distance**

	Place A	**is away from**		**Place B**	**by this much.**
	NP-place	<--distance between--> 离		NP-place	Modifier-dist.
[Example]:	美国	离		中国	很远.

Note: This very important pattern is introduced in Lesson 30 of *PCRI*. However, except for the two words 离 and 远, no other vocabulary related to this pattern is introduced at the same time. Therefore, we are going to use the words about places previously introduced to practice this pattern. Maybe it is also a good idea to learn, ahead of the class plan of the textbook, the word for "close" 近 (jin4, to appear in lesson 44 of *Practical Chinese Reader*.)

1. England is not very far away from Germany.   2. Our house is not far from the bookstore.

3. Both the bank and the library are not far from the college.

4. That factory is not far from the river.   5. The airport is not very far from my house.

6. My bedroom is too far away from the bathroom.

7. Our classroom is too close to the football stadium (...场)

8. The airplane is far from us now.

9. The exchange students are far away from home. Therefore, they are quite homesick.

10. Is the embassy farther from the center of city or from the suburb? [Use 是 ... 还是...]

Exercise XXVI (Cont.)

B. 词序 Word order: Rearrange the elements of each entry to make a grammatical sentence.

1. 离   日本   这儿   远   很

2. 很   丁太太   难过   心里

3. 他   他   笑了   很   高兴

4. 赢了   很高兴   我们   球赛   都   心里

5. 宿舍   他的   图书馆   不远   离

6. 给   女朋友   他   买了   他的   很多东西

7. 访问   我们   欢迎   你   去   国家

8. 这儿   很好   我   过得   在

9. 学习   他爸爸   努力   他   要

10. 你   好吗   送   回家   他   请

Exercise XXVI (Cont.)

C. 用词 Choice of Words: Fill in the blanks with the most appropriate words, using one character for each blank.

1. 丁国安的家＿＿＿＿ 学生宿舍很远.

2. 昨天他买 ＿＿＿＿ 一辆 (*measure for vehicles, pronounced "liang4") 车.

3. 买＿＿＿＿ 车 (以后) 他 ＿＿＿＿ 去买东西.

4. 他买＿＿＿＿ 很多＿＿＿＿ ＿＿＿＿ :他买了一 ＿＿＿＿ 鞋,两＿＿＿＿ 衬衫,
   ＿＿＿＿ 买＿＿＿＿ 一 ＿＿＿＿ 帽子.

5. 现在他有车＿＿＿＿ .＿＿＿＿ ＿＿＿＿ 去上课的时候他不要他同学来
   ＿＿＿＿ 他,他＿＿＿＿ ＿＿＿＿ 可以＿＿＿＿ 车 去＿＿＿＿ .

6. 今＿＿＿＿ 夏＿＿＿＿ 他到外国去访问＿＿＿＿ .

7. 他 ＿＿＿＿ ＿＿＿＿ 的那天,他的朋友 ＿＿＿＿ 他去机场.

8. 丁国安离＿＿＿＿ 了.他的好朋友小张 ＿＿＿＿ ＿＿＿＿ 非常＿＿＿＿ ＿＿＿＿

9. 丁国安还＿＿＿＿ 离开 ＿＿＿＿ 时候,小张 ＿＿＿＿ ＿＿＿＿ 很高兴. ＿＿＿＿
   ＿＿＿＿ 她常常＿＿＿＿ .

10. 丁国安 ＿＿＿＿ ＿＿＿＿ 以后 ,小张不常常＿＿＿＿ 了.她现在还常常
    ＿＿＿＿ . 每天都跟自＿＿＿＿ 说:"＿＿＿＿ 难过,国安就 ＿＿＿＿ ＿＿＿＿
    回来＿＿＿＿ ."

Exercise XXVI (Cont.)

D. 问答 Answering Questions: Answer the following questions according to the your real-life situations but also with the assumption that you are about to take a trip to China.

1. 机场离火车站*远吗?

2. 你家离图书馆远还是离足球场远?

3. 是大使馆(离足球场远)还是书店离足球场远?

4. 你们汉语老师的家离中文系远不远?

5. 欢送会(* farewell party) 以后,谁送老师回家?

6. 你去中国是跟老师一起去吗? 你还要去什么国家?

7. 你去中国,你爸爸妈妈放心吗?

8. 你就要离开了,谁心里很难过? 谁给你买了很多东西?

9. 你在外国的时候会很想家吗? 你会常哭吗?

10. 你什么时候回国?

Exercise XXVII
(Review L. 25-30)

A. 用词 Choice of Words: Fill in the each blank with an appropriate character to make the following two meaningful passages.

1. 明天是星期日,我想去钓鱼.我也 _____ 请我朋友跟我一起去.我给

他打 _____ 一个电话. 问他 _____ 不 _____ 去钓鱼. 我朋友说他很

_____ 去,可是他不 _____ 去,他 _____ 在家念书. 我说明天是星期

日. 我们每天都念书,很 _____. 星期日 _____ _____ 休息休息, 去

玩玩. 他说 他知道我课文 _____ 语法都会 _____ 所以我 _____ _____

去. 可是他的语法 _____ 有很多问题. 他不 _____ 去.我说我 _____

_____ 帮助他.今天晚上我 _____ _____ 跟他一起学习.他不懂的语

法我们 _____ _____ 一起研究. 他语法都懂 _____ 他 _____ _____

_____ 跟我一起去钓鱼 _____.他说,"好." 他问我 _____ 不 _____吃

_____ 晚饭 _____ 去他宿舍.我说:"好,我们 晚上 见."

2. 昨天晚上我 _____ 大友一起去王家参加 _____ 一个招待会. 晚上

六 _____ _____ 大友 _____ 车来 _____ 我. 他开车 _____ _____

很快. 十五 _____ 钟 _____ 到 _____. 所以, 我们到 _____ 很 _____.

那个招待会是为文大使开 _____ (招待会). 参加 _____ 人很多.大

家都说中国话. 大友说中国话 _____ _____ 很好.所以,他说 _____

很多 _____, _____ 认识 _____ 很多 _____ _____. 大友 _____ _____

我介绍 _____ 几 _____ 朋友. 我说中国话说 _____ 不好. 我不太

_____ 说. 我说 _____ 时候常常 _____ _____ 不对. 那些新朋友问

_____ 我很多问题, 可是我想我回答 _____ 不太 _____ _____. 我

说话 _____ _____ 不多, 可是喝酒 _____ _____ 很多. 吃菜 _____

_____ 也不 _____.王太太作菜 _____ _____ 非常 _____.招待 _____

也很 _____.我们回家 _____ _____ 很晚. 我们都玩 _____ 非

常 _____ _____.

132

Exercise XXVII (Cont.)

B. 作文 Composition: Using approximately 150 characters to write a passage discussing your plans for the future.

C. 作文 Composition: Using approximately 150 characters to write a passage about your experience of seeing off a friend at the airport.

Character Finding lists

Pinyin	Character	Lesson
à	啊	13
ài	爱	14
ān	安	29
ba	吧	21
bā	八	11
bà	爸	4
bái	白	16
bān	班	20
bàn	半	17
bàn	办	28
bāng	帮	22
bāo	包	25
bào	报	11
bēi	杯	19
bèi	备	25
běn	本	15
bǐ	笔	13
bǐ	比	28
biān	边	22
biǎo	表	23
bié	别	19
bīng	冰	28
bù	不	3
bù	步	29
cái	裁	28

Stroke #	Character	Pinyin
1	〇	líng
1	一	yī
2	八	bā
2	二	èr
2	九	jiǔ
2	了	le
2	力	lì
2	七	qī
2	人	rén
2	十	shí
2	又	yòu
2	几	jǐ
2	厂	chǎng
3	大	dà
3	大	dài
3	工	gōng
3	己	jǐ
3	口	kǒu
3	女	nǚ
3	三	sān
3	上	shàng
3	下	xià
3	小	xiǎo
3	也	yě
3	子	zǐ

Pinyin	Character	Lesson
cài	菜	27
cān	参	20
cān	餐	22
céng	层	10
chá	茶	8
chà	差	17
cháng	常	12
cháng	尝	27
chǎng	场	29
chǎng	厂	23
chàng	唱	19
chē	车	5
chèn	衬	16
chéng	城	23
chéng	成	26
chī	吃	18
chū	出	23
chú	厨	22
chuān	穿	16
chuáng	床	18
cí	词	11
cóng	从	16
cūn	村	24
cuò	错	25
dá	答	24
dǎ	打	23
dà	大	5
dài	大	5
dài	代	19
dài	待	27

Stroke#	Character	Pinyin
3	门	mén
3	飞	fēi
3	个	gè
3	干	gān
3	习	xí
3	么	me
4	不	bù
4	分	fēn
4	夫	fū
4	公	gōng
4	化	huà
4	火	huǒ
4	今	jīn
4	介	jiè
4	六	liù
4	日	rì
4	少	shǎo
4	什	shén
4	水	shuǐ
4	太	tài
4	天	tiān
4	文	wén
4	五	wǔ
4	午	wǔ
4	心	xīn
4	友	yǒu
4	月	yuè
4	中	zhōng
4	车	chē
4	见	jiàn

Pinyin	Character	Lesson		Stroke#	Character	Pinyin
dāng	当	15		4	为	wèi
dǎo	导	20		4	气	qì
dào	道	20		4	书	shū
dào	到	27		4	从	cóng
de	的	5		4	开	kāi
dé	得	25		4	认	rèn
děng	等	17		4	办	bàn
dì	弟	3		4	双	shuāng
dì	地	7		4	厅	tǐng
diǎn	典	11		5	白	bái
diǎn	点	17		5	半	bàn
diàn	店	13		5	包	bāo
diàn	电	17		5	本	běn
diào	钓	25		5	比	bǐ
dǐng	顶	28		5	出	chū
dìng	定	20		5	打	dǎ
dōng	冬	28		5	代	dài
dōng	东	30		5	冬	dōng
dǒng	懂	24		5	古	gǔ
dōu	都	3		5	互	hù
duàn	锻	24		5	加	jiā
duì	对	13		5	叫	jiào
duì	队	28		5	可	kě
duō	多	10		5	民	mín
ér	儿	10		5	片	piàn
èr	二	10		5	平	píng
fā	发	23		5	去	qù
fǎ	法	12		5	生	shēng
fān	翻	26		5	四	sì
fàn	饭	18		5	他	tā

Pinyin	Character	Lesson		Stroke#	Character	Pinyin
fáng	房	22		5	台	tái
fǎng	访	23		5	外	wài
fàng	放	29		5	以	yǐ
fēi	啡	17		5	用	yòng
fēi	非	21		5	正	zhèng
fēi	飞	29		5	左	zuǒ
fēn	分	17		5	东	dōng
fū	夫	5		5	们	men
fú	服	19		5	务	wù
fǔ	辅	20		5	队	duì
fù	复	23		5	发	fā
gāi	该	26		5	电	diàn
gān	干	27		5	号	hào
gǎn	敢	15		5	对	duì
gǎn	感	21		5	汉	hàn
gāo	高	21		5	写	xiě
gào	告	14		5	乐	yuè
gē	哥	3		5	边	biān
gē	歌	19		5	旧	jiù
gè	个	15		5	让	ràng
gěi	给	14		6	安	ān
gēn	跟	17		6	冰	bīng
gèng	更	21		6	成	chéng
gōng	工	14		6	吃	chī
gōng	公	28		6	地	dì
gū	姑	21		6	多	duō
gǔ	古	19		6	行	háng
guān	观	23		6	好	hǎo
guǎn	馆	15		6	回	huí
guì	贵	9		6	件	jiàn

Pinyin	Character	Lesson		Stroke#	Character	Pinyin
guó	国	6		6	老	lǎo
guò	过	29		6	忙	máng
hái	孩	14		6	名	míng
hái	还	19		6	奶	nǎi
hàn	汉	6		6	年	nián
háng	行	14		6	她	tā
hǎo	好	1		6	同	tóng
hào	号	10		6	西	xī
hē	喝	8		6	先	xiān
hé	和	13		6	行	xíng
hé	河	25		6	休	xiū
hè	贺	20		6	有	yǒu
hěn	很	2		6	在	zài
hóng	红	19		6	再	zài
hòu	后	17		6	早	zǎo
hòu	候	18		6	字	zì
hù	互	15		6	自	zì
huā	花	19		6	红	hóng
huá	滑	28		6	后	hòu
huà	画	11		6	师	shī
huà	话	23		6	访	fǎng
huà	化	27		6	问	wèn
huān	欢	8		6	吗	ma
huán	还	11		6	妈	mā
huí	回	17		6	买	mǎi
huì	会	20		6	当	dāng
huǒ	火	24		6	过	guò
huò	或	26		6	会	huì
jī	机	29		6	农	nóng
jǐ	几	15		6	岁	suì

Pinyin	Character	Lesson		Stroke#	Character	Pinyin
jǐ	己	30		6	团	tuán
jiā	家	14		6	导	dǎo
jiā	加	20		6	机	jī
jiān	间	22		6	兴	xīng
jiàn	见	11		6	应	yīng
jiàn	件	16		6	杂	zá
jiàn	健	27		6	欢	huān
jiào	教	15		6	观	guān
jiào	叫	9		7	吧	ba
jiào	觉	18		7	别	bié
jiē	接	23		7	步	bù
jiě	姐	14		7	床	chuáng
jiě	解	26		7	村	cūn
jiè	介	13		7	弟	dì
jīn	今	20		7	告	gào
jǐn	紧	29		7	更	gèng
jìn	进	8		7	究	jiū
jīng	京	16		7	快	kuài
jìng	竟	26		7	李	lǐ
jiū	究	26		7	没	méi
jiǔ	九	11		7	那	nà
jiǔ	酒	19		7	男	nán
jiù	旧	16		7	你	nǐ
jiù	就	26		7	努	nǔ
jú	桔	19		7	判	pàn
jù	剧	16		7	身	shēn
kā	咖	17		7	束	shù
kāi	开	21		7	忘	wàng
kàn	看	7		7	位	wèi
kāng	康	27		7	我	wǒ

Pinyin	Character	Lesson		Stroke#	Character	Pinyin
kě	可	26		7	吸	xī
kè	客	8		7	系	xì
kè	刻	17		7	找	zhǎo
kè	课	17		7	址	zhǐ
kòng	空	20		7	志	zhì
kǒu	口	15		7	住	zhù
kū	哭	30		7	助	zhu
kuài	快	25		7	走	zǒu
kuài	筷	27		7	足	zu
kuàng	矿	25		7	作	zuo
lái	来	13		7	坐	zuò
lǎn	览	15		7	来	lái
lǎo	老	6		7	两	liǎng
lào	酪	25		7	时	shí
le	了	13		7	条	tiao
lí	离	29		7	员	yuan
lǐ	理	22		7	纸	zhǐ
lǐ	里	22		7	张	zhāng
lǐ	李	28		7	这	zhe
lǐ	力	29		7	报	bào
liǎ	俩	26		7	场	chǎng
liàn	炼	24		7	词	cí
liàn	练	24		7	饭	fàn
liǎng	两	16		7	间	jiān
liang	亮	21		7	进	jìn
líng	〇	10		7	里	lǐ
líng	零	10		7	诉	sù
liu	留	9		7	汤	tāng
liù	六	11		7	园	yuan
lou	楼	27		7	远	yuǎn

Pinyin	Character	Lesson		Stroke#	Character	Pinyin
lù	路	29		7	层	céng
lǜ	绿	16		7	还	huán
ma	吗	2		7	识	shì
mā	妈	4		7	证	zhèng
mǎi	买	13		7	译	yì
màn	慢	25		7	听	tīng
máng	忙	3		7	体	tǐ
máo	茅	27		8	爸	bà
mào	帽	28		8	杯	bēi
me	么	7		8	表	biǎo
méi	没	14		8	到	dào
měi	每	18		8	的	de
mèi	妹	14		8	典	diǎn
men	们	3		8	店	diàn
mén	门	21		8	定	dìng
miàn	面	22		8	儿	ér
miàn	面	25		8	房	fáng
mín	民	19		8	放	fàng
míng	名	13		8	法	fǎ
míng	明	23		8	非	fēi
nǎ	哪	6		8	服	fú
nà	那	5		8	姑	gū
nǎi	奶	25		8	和	hé
nán	男	13		8	河	hé
nán	难	24		8	花	huā
ne	呢	2		8	或	huò
néng	能	26		8	姐	jiě
nǐ	你	1		8	京	jīng
nián	年	20		8	咖	kā
niàn	念	24		8	刻	kè

Pinyin	Character	Lesson		Stroke#	Character	Pinyin
niáng	娘	21		8	空	kòng
nín	您	8		8	每	měi
nóng	农	24		8	妹	mèi
nǔ	努	29		8	明	míng
nǚ	女	12		8	呢	ne
pàn	判	28		8	念	niàn
páng	旁	22		8	朋	péng
péng	朋	4		8	衫	shān
pí	啤	19		8	舍	shè
piàn	片	23		8	始	shǐ
piào	票	16		8	使	shǐ
piào	漂	21		8	事	shì
píng	瓶	19		8	所	suǒ
píng	平	28		8	玩	wán
pú	葡	27		8	些	xiē
qī	七	11		8	姓	xìng
qī	期	20		8	易	yì
qǐ	起	17		8	迎	yíng
qì	气	8		8	泳	yǒng
qiān	签	28		8	招	zhāo
qián	前	25		8	者	zhě
qīng	轻	21		8	知	zhī
qíng	情	30		8	注	zhù
qǐng	请	8		8	英	yīng
qiū	秋	29		8	参	cān
qiú	球	28			钓	diào
qù	去	12		8	顶	dǐng
quán	泉	26		8	国	guó
qún	裙	16		8	绍	shào
ràng	让	19		8	视	shì

Pinyin	Character	Lesson		Stroke#	Character	Pinyin
rè	热	30		8	现	xiàn
rén	人	6		8	鱼	yú
rèn	认	12		8	备	bèi
rì	日	20		8	画	huà
róng	容	26		8	该	gāi
sài	赛	28		8	话	huà
sān	三	10		8	试	shì
shān	衫	16		8	图	tú
shāng	商	13		8	练	liàn
shàng	上	16		8	学	xue
shǎo	少	10		8	矿	kuàng
shao	绍	13		8	衬	chèn
shè	舍	10		9	城	chéng
shei	谁	6		9	待	dài
shēn	深	26		9	孩	hái
shēn	身	29		9	很	hěn
shen	什	7		9	看	kàn
shēng	生	9		9	客	kè
shī	师	6		9	亮	liang
shí	十	11		9	茅	mao
shí	食	17		9	面	miàn
shí	时	18		9	前	qiàn
shǐ	始	27		9	秋	qiū
shǐ	使	27		9	泉	quan
shì	是	4		9	食	shí
shì	识	12		9	是	shì
shì	室	15		9	室	shì
shì	事	17		9	思	sī
shì	视	23		9	卧	wò
shì	试	27		9	洗	xǐ

Pinyin	Character	Lesson		**Stroke#**	Character	Pinyin
shū	书	5		9	相	xiāng
shū	输	28		9	相	xiàng
shù	束	21		9	信	xìn
shuāng	双	28		9	星	xīng
shuǐ	水	19		9	要	yào
shuì	睡	18		9	音	yīn
shuō	说	13		9	怎	zěn
sī	思	20		9	祝	zhù
sì	四	10		9	昨	zuó
sòng	送	21		9	俩	liǎ
sù	宿	10		9	研	yán
sù	诉	14		9	复	fù
suì	岁	20		9	给	gěi
suǒ	所	29		9	贵	guì
tā	他	3		9	贺	hè
tā	她	5		9	炼	liàn
tái	台	27		9	尝	cháng
tài	太	16		9	轻	qīng
tán	谈	26		9	说	shuō
tāng	汤	25		9	闻	wén
táng	堂	17		9	语	yǔ
táo	萄	27		9	点	diǎn
tī	踢	28		9	总	zǒng
tí	题	18		9	觉	jiào
tǐ	体	29		9	面	miàn
tiān	天	18		9	览	lǎn
tiáo	条	16		10	班	bān
tiào	跳	21		10	茶	chá
tīng	听	19		10	差	chà
tīng	厅	22		10	穿	chuān

Pinyin	Character	Lesson	Stroke#	Character	Pinyin
tíng	停	25	10	高	gāo
tóng	同	20	10	哥	gē
tu	图	7	10	候	hòu
tuán	团	23	10	家	jiā
tuǐ	腿	25	10	酒	jiǔ
wài	外	9	10	哭	kū
wán	玩	23	10	留	liú
wǎn	晚	16	10	哪	nǎ
wàng	忘	29	10	能	néng
wèi	喂	13	10	娘	niang
wèi	位	25	10	旁	páng
wèi	为	27	10	起	qǐ
wén	文	15	10	容	róng
wén	闻	23	10	送	sòng
wèn	问	9	10	息	xí
wǒ	我	2	10	夏	xià
wò	卧	22	10	笑	xiào
wǔ	五	10	10	烟	yān
wǔ	午	18	10	院	yuàn
wǔ	舞	20	10	站	zhàn
wù	务	19	10	真	zhēn
xī	吸	8	10	桌	zhuō
xī	西	30	10	笔	bǐ
xí	习	9	10	准	zhǔn
xí	息	18	10	爱	ài
xǐ	喜	19	10	准	zhǔn
xǐ	洗	22	10	紧	jǐn
xì	系	15	10	剧	jù
xià	下	11	10	课	kè
xià	夏	29	10	请	qǐng

Pinyin	Character	Lesson		Stroke#	Character	Pinyin
xiān	先	12		10	热	rè
xiàn	现	11		10	谁	shéi
xiāng	相	15		10	谈	tán
xiāng	箱	28		10	样	yàng
xiǎng	想	14		10	谊	yì
xiàng	相	21		10	阅	yuè
xiàng	象	21		10	桔	jú
xiǎo	小	19		10	帮	bāng
xiào	笑	30		10	离	lí
xiē	些	24		10	难	nán
xié	鞋	28		11	啊	à
xiě	写	14		11	常	cháng
xiè	谢	8		11	唱	chàng
xīn	新	15		11	得	dé
xīn	心	24		11	都	dōu
xìn	信	14		11	啡	fēi
xīng	星	20		11	健	jiàn
xìng	姓	9		11	教	jiao
xìng	兴	21		11	接	jiē
xiū	休	18		11	竟	jìng
xué	学	9		11	康	kāng
yān	烟	8		11	理	lǐ
yán	研	26		11	您	nín
yàng	样	22		11	啤	pí
yào	要	19		11	票	piào
yě	也	2		11	瓶	píng
yī	一	10		11	情	qíng
yǐ	以	17		11	球	qiú
yǐ	椅	22		11	商	shāng
yì	意	20		11	深	shēn

Pinyin	Character	Lesson		Stroke#	Character	Pinyin
yì	译	26		11	宿	sù
yì	易	26		11	堂	táng
yì	谊	27		11	停	tíng
yīn	音	19		11	晚	wǎn
yín	银	14		11	爲	wèi
yīng	英	12		11	辅	fǔ
yìng	应	26		11	银	yín
yíng	迎	8		11	绿	lǜ
yíng	赢	28		11	馆	guǎn
yǐng	影	17		12	裁	cái
yǒng	泳	25		12	菜	cài
yòng	用	11		12	答	dá
yóu	游	25		12	等	děng
yǒu	友	4		12	敢	gǎn
yǒu	有	14		12	喝	hē
yòu	又	27		12	就	jiù
yú	鱼	25		12	帽	mào
yǔ	语	6		12	期	qī
yuán	员	19		12	裙	qún
yuán	园	22		12	萄	táo
yuǎn	远	30		12	喂	wèi
yuàn	院	9		12	喜	xǐ
yuàn	愿	29		12	椅	yǐ
yuè	阅	15		12	游	yóu
yuè	乐	19		12	象	xiàng
yuè	月	20		12	谢	xiè
zá	杂	15		13	道	dào
zài	在	10		13	感	gǎn
zài	再	11		13	跟	gēn
zàn	赞	27		13	滑	huá

Pinyin	Character	Lesson		Stroke#	Character	Pinyin
zǎo	澡	22		13	解	jiě
zǎo	早	26		13	筷	kuài
zěn	怎	22		13	酪	lào
zhàn	站	29		13	零	líng
zhāng	张	16		13	路	lù
zhāo	招	27		13	葡	pú
zhǎo	找	16		13	跳	tiào
zhao	照	23		13	想	xiǎng
zhě	者	26		13	新	xīn
zhe	这	4		13	意	yì
zhēn	真	21		13	照	zhao
zhěng	整	22		13	楼	lóu
zheng	正	23		13	错	cuò
zheng	证	28		13	输	shū
zhī	知	20		13	签	qiān
zhǐ	纸	13		14	歌	gē
zhǐ	址	20		14	慢	màn
zhì	志	15		14	漂	piào
zhì	志	26		14	睡	shuì
zhōng	中	15		14	腿	tuǐ
zhù	住	10		14	志	zhì
zhù	祝	20		14	锻	duàn
zhù	助	22		14	赛	sài
zhù	注	29		14	愿	yuàn
zhǔn	准	25		15	厨	chú
zhuō	桌	22		15	踢	tī
zǐ	子	14		15	舞	wǔ
zì	字	13		15	箱	xiāng
zì	自	30		15	鞋	xié
zǒng	总	22		15	影	yǐng

Pinyin	Character	Lesson		Stroke#	Character	Pinyin
zǒu	走	17		15	题	tí
zú	足	28		16	餐	cān
zuó	昨	28		16	懂	dǒng
zuǒ	左	22		16	澡	zǎo
zuò	坐	10		16	整	zhěng
zuò	作	14		16	赞	zàn
				17	赢	yíng
				18	翻	fān

Character Conversion Table

Lesson	2	3	4	5		6			
Simplified	吗	们	这	妈	车	书	国	谁	师	汉
Traditional	嗎	們	這	媽	車	書	國	誰	師	漢

Lesson	6	7		8					9
Simplified	语	什	么	图	请	进	欢	谢	气	贵
Traditional	語	甚	麼	圖	請	進	歡	謝	氣	貴

Lesson	9			10		11			
Simplified	问	学	习	儿	号	层	还	画	报	词
Traditional	問	學	習	兒	號	層	還	畫	報	詞

Lesson	11		12		13				
Simplified	现	见	认	识	英	买	笔	纸	来	绍
Traditional	現	見	認	識	英	買	筆	紙	來	紹

Lesson	13		14					15	
Simplified	对	说	银	爱	给	写	诉	个	几	当
Traditional	對	說	銀	愛	給	寫	訴	個	幾	當

Lesson	15				16				
Simplified	阅	览	杂	志	馆	条	两	张	剧	从
Traditional	閱	覽	雜	誌	館	條	兩	張	劇	從

Lesson	16		17			18			
Simplified	旧	衬	绿	点	课	后	电	饭	时	题
Traditional	舊	襯	綠	點	課	後	電	飯	時	題

Lesson	18	19						20	
Simplified	觉	务	员	红	桔	听	乐	让	辅	导
Traditional	覺	務	員	紅	橘	聽	樂	讓	輔	導

Lesson	20			21				22	
Simplified	岁	贺	会	参	兴	轻	开	门	边	园
Traditional	歲	賀	會	參	興	輕	開	門	邊	園

Lesson	22				23				
Simplified	厅	总	帮	里	间	样	视	话	复	闻
Traditional	廳	總	幫	裏	間	樣	視	話	復	聞

Lesson	23				24				
Simplified	团	观	厂	访	发	农	锻	炼	难	练
Traditional	團	觀	廠	訪	發	農	鍛	煉	難	練

Lesson	**25**								**26**
Simplified	准	备	钓	鱼	汤	错	面	矿	研	谈
Traditional	準	備	釣	魚	湯	錯	麵	礦	研	談

Lesson	**26**				**27**				
Simplified	译	应	该	俩	尝	为	干	谊	试	赞
Traditional	譯	應	該	倆	嘗	爲	乾	誼	試	贊

Lesson	**27**	**28**							
Simplified	楼	赛	办	签	证	队	赢	输	顶	双
Traditional	樓	賽	辦	簽	證	隊	贏	輸	頂	雙

Lesson	**29**								**30**
Simplified	飞	机	场	愿	离	紧	体	过	东	热
Traditional	飛	機	場	願	離	緊	體	過	東	熱

Lesson	**30**
Simplified	远
Traditional	遠

PCR I Vocabulary

Lesson Sequence

Lesson	Pinyin	Characters	Function	English meaning
1	hǎo	好	adj, v-state	good, to be good, to be well
1	nǐ	你	pron	you
1*	Gǔbō	古波	n-prop	Gubo
1*	Pàlánkǎ	帕兰卡	prop	Palanka
2	hěn	很	adv	very
2	ma	吗	particle	an interrogative particle
2	ne	呢	particle	a modal particle
2	wǒ	我	pron	I, me
2	yě	也	adv	also, too
3	bù	不	adv	not, no
3	dìdi	弟弟	n	younger brother
3	dōu	都	adv	all
3	gēge	哥哥	n	elder brother
3	máng	忙	adj. v-state	busy, to be busy
3	tā	他	pron	he, him
3	tāmen	们	pron	they, them
4	bàba	爸爸	n	father
4	māma	妈妈	n	mother
4	nǐmen	你们	pron	you (pl.)
4	péngyou	朋友	n	friend
4	shì	是	v-id	to be

Note: * = Proper Noun
　　　　　 ** = Supplementary word

153

Lesson	Pinyin	Characters	Function	English meaning
4	zhè	这	pron	this
5	chē	车	n	car
5	dàifu	大夫	n	doctor
5	de	的	particle	a structural particle
5	nà	那	pron	that
5	shū	书	n	book
5	tā	她	pron	she, her
5**	bào	报	n	newspaper
5**	bǐ	笔	n	pen, pencil, brush-pen
5**	chǐ	尺	n	ruler
5**	zhǐ	纸	n	paper
6	guó	国	n	country, state
6	Hànyǔ	汉语	n	Chinese (language)
6	lǎo	老	adj., v-state	old, to be old
6	lǎoshī	老师	n	teacher
6	nǎ	哪	pron	which
6	rén	人	n	person
6	shéi	谁	pron	who
6	wǒmen	我们	pron	we, us
6*	Zhōngguó	中国	n-prop	China
6**	Déguó	德国	n-prop	Germany
6**	Fǎguó	法国	n-prop	France
6**	Mǎlǐ	马里	n-prop	Mali
6**	Měiguó	美国	n-prop	U.S.A.
6**	Rìběn	日本	n-prop	Japan
7	dìtú	地图	n	map, atlas
7	kàn	看	v-act	to look, to read, to watch
7	shénme	什么	pron	what
7*	Běijīng	北京	n-prop	Beijing
7*	Chángjiāng	长江	n-prop	The Yangtze River
7*	Huáng Hé	黄河	n-prop	The Yellow River

Lesson	Pinyin	Characters	Function	English meaning
7*	Shànghǎi	上海	n-prop	Shanghai
7*	Chángchéng	长城	n-prop	The Great Wall
7**	Dàyáng Zhōu	大洋洲	n-prop	Oceania
7**	Fēi Zhōu	非洲	n-prop	Africa
7**	Nán Měi Zhōu	南美洲	n-prop	South America
7**	Ōu Zhōu	欧洲	n-prop	Europe
7**	shìjiè	世界	n	world
8	chá	茶	n	tea
8	hē	喝	v-act	to drink
8	huānyíng	欢迎	v-act	to welcome
8	jìn	进	v-act	to enter, to come in
8	kèqi	客气	adj, v-state	polite, to be polite
8	nín	您	pron	polite form of "nǐ"
8	qǐng	请	v-act	please
8	xī yān	吸煙(烟)	v-act	to smoke
8	yān	煙(烟)	n	cigarette
8	xièxie	谢谢	v-act	to thank
8*	Wáng	王	n-prop	Wang
8**	kāfēi	咖啡	n	coffee
8**	niúnǎi	牛奶	n	milk
8**	píjiǔ	啤酒	n	beer
8**	tàitai	太太	n	Mrs., madame
8**	xiānsheng	先生	n	Mr., sir, gentleman
9	guì xìng	贵姓	idiom	What's your name?
9	jiào	叫	v-id	to call, to be called
9	líuxuéshēng	留学生	n	a foreign student
9	qǐngwèn	请问	idiom	May I ask...?
9	wàiyǔ	外语	n	foreign language
9	wèn	问	v-act	to ask
9	xìng	姓	n, v-id	a surname, (one's) surname is...
9	xué	学	v	to study, to learn

Lesson	Pinyin	Characters	Function	English meaning
9	xuésheng	学生	n	student
9	xuéxí	学习	v	to study, to learn
9	xuéyuàn	学院	n	college, institute
9*	Dīng Yún	丁云	n-prop	Ding Yun
9**	Cháoxiǎn	朝鲜	n-prop	Korea
9**	nǚshì	女士	n	polite address to a lady
9**	tóngzhì	同志	n	comrade
9**	xiǎojie	小姐	n	miss
9**	Yīngguó	英国	n-prop	Britain
10	céng	层	measure	story (of a building)
10	duōshao	多少	pron	how many, how much
10	èr	二	number	two
10	hào	号	n	number
10	líng	零	number	zero
10	nǎr	哪儿	pron	where
10	sān	三	number	three
10	sì	四	number	four
10	sùshè	宿舍	n	dormitory
10	wǔ	五	number	five
10	yī	一	number	one
10	zài	在	v-loc	to be at, to be in
10	zhù	住	v-loc	to live
10	zuò	坐	v-act	to sit, to take a seat
10**	cèsuǒ	厕所	n	toilet, lavatory
10**	nàr	那儿	pron	there
10**	yīyuàn	医院	n	hospital
10**	zhèr	这儿	pron	here
11	bā	八	number	eight
11	cídiǎn	词典	n	dictionary
11	huàbào	画报	n	pictorial

Lesson	Pinyin	Characters	Function	English meaning
11	huán	还	v-act	to return
11	jiǔ	九	number	nine
11	liù	六	number	six
11	qī	七	number	seven
11	shí	十	number	ten
11	xiànzài	现在	n-time	now, nowadays
11	yíxiàr	一下儿	idiom	a little while
11	yòng	用	v-act	to use, to make use of
11	zàijiàn	再见	idiom	See you again; Good bye
11**	běnzi	本子	n	note-book
11**	diànhuà	电话	n	telephone, telephone call
11**	yǔsǎn	雨伞	n	umbrella
11**	zázhì	杂志	n	magazine
12	cháng	常	adv	often
12	Fǎyǔ	法语	n	French
12	nǚ	女	adj	female
12	qù	去	v-act	to go
12	rènshi	认识	v-cog	to know, to recognize
12	tāmen	她们	pron	they, them (for females)
12	xiānsheng	先生	n	Mr., sir, gentleman
12	Yīngyǔ	英语	n	English
13	à	啊	interj	oh
13	bǐ	笔	n	pen
13	duì	对	v-state	to be right, to be correct
13	hé	和	conj	and, with
13	jièshào	介绍	v-act	to introduce
13	lái	来	v-act	to come
13	le	了	particle	a modal particle
13	mǎi	买	v-act	to buy
13	míngzi	名	n	name
13	nán	男	adj	male

Lesson	Pinyin	Characters	Function	English meaning
13	shāngdiàn	商店	n	shop
13	shuō	说	v-act	to speak, to say
13	wèi	喂	interj	hello
13	zhǐ	纸	n	paper
13*	Dīng Yún	丁云	n-prop	Ding Yun
13*	Gǔbō	古波	n-prop	Gubo
13*	Pàlánkǎ	帕兰卡	n-prop	Palanka
13*	Zhōngguó	中国	n-prop	China
13**	běnzi	本子	n	note-book
13**	Fǎguó	法国	n-prop	France
13**	jiàoshòu	教授	n	professor
13**	Yīngguó	英国	n-prop	Britain
13**	yóujú	邮局	n	post office
13**	yóupiào	邮票	n	stamp
14	àiren	爱人	n	spouse
14	gàosu	告诉	v-act	to tell
14	gěi	给	co-v, v-act	to, for, to give
14	gōngzuò	工作	n, v-act	work, to work
14	háizi	孩子	n	child
14	jiā	家	n	family, home, house
14	jiějie	姐姐	n	elder sister
14	méi	没	adv, v-poss	not, no, do not have
14	mèimei	妹妹	n	younger sister
14	shūdiàn	书店	n	bookstore
14	xiǎng	想	v-act, v-int	to think, to miss, to want
14	xiě	写	v-act	to write
14	xìn	信	n	letter
14	yínháng	银行	n	bank
14	yǒu	有	v-poss	to have, there be
14	zuò	作	v-act	to do
14**	gōngchéngshī	工程师	n	engineer

Lesson	Pinyin	Characters	Function	English meaning
14**	gōngsī	公司	n	company
14**	jīnglǐ	经理	n	manager, director
14**	zhíyuán	职员	n	office worker, staff
15	bào	报	n	newspaper
15	běn	本	measure	volume
15	bù gǎndāng	不敢当	idiom	I don't really deserve it.
15	ge	个	measure	a measure word
15	hái	还	adv	still, in addition, else
15	Hànzì	汉字	n	Chinese character
15	hùxiāng	互相	adv	each other, mutually
15	jǐ	几	pron/numb.	how many, how much, several
15	jiāo	教	v-act	to teach
15	kǒuyǔ	口语	n	spoken language
15	nàr	那儿	pron	there
15	túshūguǎn	图书馆	n	library
15	xì	系	n	department, faculty
15	xīn	新	adj, v-state	new, to be new
15	yǔfǎ	语法	n	grammar
15	yuèlǎnshì	阅览室	n	reading room
15	zázhì	杂志	n	magazine
15	Zhōngwén	中文	n	Chinese (language)
15	zì	字	n	character
15*	Wáng	王	n-prop	Wang
15**	bān	班	n	class, squad
15**	jiàoshì	教室	n	classroom
15**	jiè	借	v-act	to borrow, to lend
15**	shēngcí	生词	n	new word
15**	shíyànshì	实验室	n	laboratory
16	bái	白	adj, v-state	white, to be white
16	chènshān	衬衫	n	shirt, blouse
16	chuān	穿	v-act	to put on, to wear

Lesson	Pinyin	Characters	Function	English meaning
16	cóng	从	co-v	from
16	dà	大	adj, v-state	big, large, to be big, to be large
16	jiàn	件	measure	a measure word
16	jīngjù	京剧	n	Beijing opera
16	jiù	旧	adj, v-state	old, to be old
16	liǎng	两	number	two
16	lǜ	绿	adj, v-state	green, to be green
16	piào	票	n	ticket
16	qúnzi	裙子	n	skirt
16	tài	太	adv	too, too much
16	tiáo	条	measure	a measure word
16	wǎnshang	晚上	n	evening
16	zhāng	张	measure	piece
16	zhǎo	找	v-act	to look for, to call on (a person)
16	zhèr	这儿	pron	here
16**	dàyī	大衣	n	overcoat, topcoat
16**	hēi	黑	adj, v-state	black, to be black
16**	jùchǎng	剧场	n	theatre
16**	kùzi	裤子	n	trousers
16**	lán	蓝	adj, v-state	blue, to be blue
16**	shàngyī	上衣	n	upper outer garment
16**	zuòwèi	座位	n	seat
17	a	啊	particle	Ah, (a modal particle)
17	bàn	半	number	half
17	chà	差	v-state	to be short of, to lack
17	kāfēiguǎn	咖啡馆	n	cafe
17	děng	等	v-act	to wait
17	diǎn	点	measure	o'clock, point
17	diànyǐng	电影	n	film, movie
17	fēn	分	measure	minute
17	gēn	跟	co-v, v	with, to follow

Lesson	Pinyin	Characters	Function	English meaning
17	huí	回	v-act	to return
17	kāfēi	咖啡	n	coffee
17	kè	刻	measure	quarter (or an hour)
17	kè	课	n	class
17	lù	路	n	road, way
17	shàng(kè)	上课	v-act	to attend or to teach (a class)
17	shítáng	食堂	n	dining-hall
17	shìr	事儿	n	business, thing
17	xià(kè)	下课	v-act	class is over or dismissed
17	yǐhòu	以后	n	later on, in the future
17	yìqǐ	一起	adv	together
17	zǒu	走	v-act	to go, to walk
17**	biǎo	表	n	watch
17**	diànyǐngyuàn	电影院	n	cinema
17**	shàng bān	上班	idiom	to go to work
17**	xià bān	下班	idiom	to come or go off work
17**	yǐqián	以前	n-time	before, in the past, ago
17**	zhōng	钟	n	clock
18	chī	吃	v-act	to eat
18	chuáng	床	n	bed
18	duō	多	adj, v-state	many, much, a lot of
18	fàn	饭	n	meal, cooked rice, food
18	měi	每	pron	every, each
18	qǐ	起	v-act	to get up, to rise
18	qǐ chuáng	起床	idiom	to get up
18	shàngwǔ	上午	n-time	morning
18	shuì jiào	睡觉	idiom	to go to bed, to sleep
18	tiān	天	n	day
18	wèntí	问题	n	question
18	xiàwǔ	下午	n-time	afternoon
18	xiūxi	休息	v-act	to take a rest

Lesson	Pinyin	Characters	Function	English meaning
18	yǒu shíhou	有时候	idiom	sometimes
18*	Běijīng	北京	n-prop	Beijing
19	bēi	杯	measure	cup
19	bié	别	adv	don't
19	chàng	唱	v-act	to sing
19	fúwùyuán	服务员	n	waiter, waitress, attendant
19	gēr	歌儿	n	song
19	gǔdiǎn	古典	n	classical, classic
19	háishì	还是	conj	or
19	hóng	红	adj, v-state	red, to be red
19	hóngchá	红茶	n	black tea
19	huāchá	花茶	n	scented tea, jasmine tea
19	júzi	桔子	n	orange
19	júzishuǐ	桔子水	n	orangeade, orange juice
19	míngē	民歌	n	folk song
19	píjiǔ	啤酒	n	beer
19	píng	瓶	measure	bottle
19	ràng	让	v-act	to let, to ask
19	shuǐ	水	n	water
19	tīng	听	v-act	to listen
19	xǐhuan	喜欢	v-act	to like, to be fond of
19	xiàndài	现代	n	modern
19	xiǎojie	小姐	n	miss, young lady
19	yào	要	v-int, v-act	must, to be going to, to want
19	yīnyuè	音乐	n	music
19**	chàngpiàn	唱片	n	gramophone record
19**	lǜchá	绿茶	n	green tea
19**	píngguǒ	苹果	n	apple
19**	pútao	葡萄	n	grape
19**	táng	糖	n	sugar, sweets, candy

Lesson	Pinyin	Characters	Function	English meaning
19**	xiāngjiāo	香蕉	n	banana
19**	zhī	枝	measure	branch, etc.
20	bān	班	n	class, squad
20	cānjiā	参加	v-act	to take part in, to attend
20	dìzhǐ	地址	n	address
20	fǔdǎo	辅导	v-act	to coach
20	hào	号	n	date, day of the month
20	jīnnián	今年	n	this year
20	jīntiān	今天	n	today
20	kòngr	空儿	n	spare time
20	nián	年	n	year
20	rì	日	n	date, day of the month
20	shēngrì	生日	n	birthday
20	suì	岁	measure	year (age)
20	tóngxué	同学	n	classmate, schoolmate
20	wǔhuì	舞会	n	dance, ball
20	xīngqī	星期	n	week
20	xīngqīrì	星期日	n	Sunday
20	yídìng	一定	adj, adv	particular, surely, certainly
20	yǒu yìsi	有意思	adj-comb	interesting
20	yuè	月	n	month
20	zhīdao	知道	v-cog	to know
20	zhùhè	祝贺	n, v-act	congratulation, to congratulate
20**	duì bu qǐ	对不起	idiom	I'm sorry
20**	jié hūn	结婚	v-comb	to get married
20**	méi guānxi	没关系	idiom	it doesn't matter
20**	míngnián	明年	n	next year
20**	qùnián	去年	n	last year
20**	tán	谈	v-act	to talk, to chat
20**	yīnyuèhuì	音乐会	n	concert

Lesson	Pinyin	Characters	Function	English meaning
20**	yuēhuì	约会	n	appointment
21	ba	吧	particle	(a modal particle)
21	duō	多	adv	how
21	fēicháng	非常	adv	extremely
21	gǎnxiè	感谢	v-act	to thank
21	gāoxìng	高兴	adj, v-state	happy, to be glad, to be delighted
21	gèng	更	adv	even, still
21	gūniang	姑娘	n	girl
21	hǎokàn	好看	adj, v-state	good-looking, to be pretty
21	huār	花儿	n	flower
21	kāi	开	v-act	to open
21	mén	门	n	door
21	niánqīng	年轻	adj, v-state	young, to be young
21	piàoliang	漂亮	adj. v-state	pretty, to be pretty, (to be) beautiful
21	shù	束	measure	bunch
21	sòng	送	v-act	to give, to give as a present
21	tàitai	太太	n	Mrs., madame
21	tiào wǔ	跳舞	v-comb	to dance
21	xiàng	象	v-id	to be like, to resemble
21	zhēn	真	adj	real, true, genuine
21	zhù	祝	v-act	to wish
21*	Bùlǎng	布朗	n-prop	Brown, a personal name
21*	Rìběn	日本	n-prop	Japan
21**	érzi	儿子	n	son
21**	gānjing	干净	adj, v-state	clean, neat, to be clean, to be neat
21**	lǐwù	礼物	n	present, gift
21**	liàng	辆	measure	measure word for vehicle
21**	nǚ ér	女儿	n	daughter
21**	suìshu	岁数	n	age
21**	xīnnián	新年	n	New Year

164

Lesson	Pinyin	Characters	Function	English meaning
21**	zhàopiàn	照片	n	photograph, picture
22	bāng	帮	v-act	to help
22	bāngzhu	帮助	n, v-act	help, to help
22	cāntīng	餐厅	n	dining-hall
22	chúfáng	厨房	n	kitchen
22	duìmiàn	对面	n	opposite
22	fángjiān	房间	n	room
22	fángzi	房子	n	house
22	hòubiān	后边	n	back, at the back of, behind
22	huāyuán	花园	n	garden
22	kètīng	客厅	n	drawing room, parlour
22	lǐbiān	里边	n	inside
22	pángbiān	旁边	n	side
22	shàngbiān	上边	n	top, on, over, above
22	shǎo	少	adj, v-state	few, little, to be few, to be little
22	shūfáng	书房	n	study
22	wòshì	卧室	n	bedroom
22	xǐ zǎo	洗澡	v-act	to take a bath
22	xǐzǎojiān	洗澡间	n	bathroom
22	xiǎo	小	adj, v-state	little, small, to be little, to be small
22	yǐzi	椅子	n	chair
22	zěnmeyàng	怎么样	idiom	how is it
22	zhěnglǐ	整理	v-act	to put in order, to straighten up
22	zhuōzi	桌子	n	table
22	zǒng	总	adv	always
22	zǒngshì	总是	adv	always
22	zuǒbiān	左边	n	left
22**	bǎ	把	measure	measure word
22**	chuānghu	窗户	n	window
22**	qiánbiān	前边	n	front, in front of, before
22**	tào	套	measure	set

Lesson	Pinyin	Characters	Function	English meaning
22**	wàibiān	外边	n	outside
22**	xiàbiān	下边	n	bottom
22**	yòubiān	右边	n	right
22**	zhōngjiān	中间	n	middle
23	cānguān	参观	v-act	to visit, to pay a visit
23	chéng	城	n	city, town
23	chūfā	出发	v-act	to start out, to set off
23	dǎ (diànhuà)	打(电话)	v-act	to make (a telephone call)
23	dàibiǎo	代表	n	delegate, representative
23	dàibiǎotuán	代表团	n	delegation
23	diànhuà	电话	n	telephone, telephone call
23	diànshì	电视	n	television
23	fǎngwèn	访问	v-act	to visit, to call on
23	fùxí	复习	v-act	to review
23	gōngchǎng	工厂	n	factory
23	gōngrén	工人	n	worker
23	yǒuhǎo	友好	v-state	to be friendly
23	jiē (diànhuà)	接(电话)	v-act	to answer (the phone)
23	jiē (rén)	接(人)	ve-act	to meet (a person)
23	kāi (chē)	开(车)	v-act	to drive (a car)
23	kèwén	课文	n	text
23	méi (you)	没(有)	adv	not, no
23	míngtiān	明天	n	tomorrow
23	wàibiān	外边	n	outside
23	wánr	玩儿	v-act	to play, to have fun with
23	xīnwén	新闻	n	news
23	yǒuhǎo	友好	adj	friendly
23	zhàopiàn	照片	n	photograph, photo, picture
23	zhèngzài	正在	adv	(action in progress)
23*	Rénmín Rìbào	人民日报	n-prop	The People's Daily

Lesson	Pinyin	Characters	Function	English meaning
23**	dǎ cuò le	打错了	idiom	you (or I)'ve dialled the wrong #
23**	fēnjī	分机	n	extension
23**	hàomǎ	号码	n	number
23**	zhàn xiàn	占线	idiom	the line is busy
23**	zǒngjī	总机	n	central exchange, switchboard
24	cí	词	n	word
24	diǎnxin	点心	n	light refreshments, pastry
24	dǒng	懂	v-cog	to understand
24	duànliàn	锻炼	v-act	to do physical training
24	huídá	回答	v-act	to reply, to answer
24	huǒchē	火车	n	train
24	liànxí	练习	n, v-act	exercise, to practice
24	nán	难	adj, v-state	difficult, to be difficult
24	niàn	念	v-act	to read (aloud), to study
24	nóngcūn	农村	n	countryside, rural areas
24	nóngmín	农民	n	peasant
24	rènzhēn	认真	adj, v-state	(to be) conscientious /serious
24	shēngcí	生词	n	new word
24	xiē	些	m	some
24*	Ānnà	安娜	n-prop	Anna
24*	Wáng Shūwén	王书文	n-prop	Wang Shuwen
25	búcuò	不错	adj	correct, not bad, pretty good
25	de	得	particle	particle, structural
25	diào	钓	v-act	to fish with a hook and bait
25	hé	河	n	river
25	huǒtuǐ	火腿	n	ham
25	jiàoliàn	教练	n	coach, trainer
25	kuài	快	adj	fast, quick
25	kuàngquánshuǐ	矿泉水	n	mineral water
25	màn	慢	adj	slow
25	miànbāo	面包	n	bread

Lesson	Pinyin	Characters	Function	English meaning
25	nǎli	哪里	idiom	it is nothing
25	nǎilào	奶酪	n	cheese
25	qiánbiān	前边	n	front
25	tāng	汤	n	soup
25	tíng	停	v-act	to stop, to come to a stop
25	wǎn	晚	adj	late
25	wèi	位	measure	measure word
25	yìdiǎnr	一点儿	idiom	a little, a bit
25	yóu yǒng	游泳	v-comb	to swim, swimming
25	yú	鱼	n	fish
25	zài	再	adv	again, once more
25	zhǔnbèi	准备	v-act	to prepare
25**	bǐjiào	比较	adv, v-act	comparatively, to compare
25**	cài	菜	n	dish
25**	jīdàn	鸡蛋	n	hen's egg
25**	jiǎozi	饺子	n	Chinese dumpling
25**	liúli	流利	adj	fluent
25**	niúnǎi	牛奶	n	milk (cows)
25**	qīngchu	清楚	adj	clear, distinct
25**	zhěngqí	整齐	adj, v-state	tidy, to be tidy
26	chéngyǔ	成语	n	proverb, idiom
26	dāng	当	v-id	to act as, to serve as
26	fānyì	翻译	n, v-act	interpreter, to interpret / translate
26	huì	会	v-cog	to know how to, can
26	huòzhě	或者	conj	or
26	jiāshēn	加深	v-act	to deepen
26	jiù	就	adv, conj	at once, right away, then
26	kěshì	可是	conj	but
26	kěyǐ	可以	aux. v	may
26	lǐxiǎng	理想	n, adj	ideal
26	liǎ	俩	m	both, two

Lesson	Pinyin	Characters	Function	English meaning
26	liǎojiě	了解	v-cog	to understand, to know
26	néng	能	v-cog	can, to be able to
26	rénmín	人民	n	people
26	róngyì	容易	adj	easy
26	tán	谈	v-act	to talk, to chat
26	wénxué	文学	n	literature
26	yánjiū	研究	n, v-act	research, to research, to study
26	yīnggāi	应该	?aux. v	should, ought to
26	yǒumíng	有名	adj	famous, well-known
26	zǎo	早	adj	early
26	zuòjiā	作家	n	writer
26*	Guō Mòruò	郭沫若	n-prop	Guo Moruo
26*	Lǔ Xùn	鲁迅	n-prop	Lu Xun
26**	gējù	歌剧	n	opera
26**	huà	画	v-act	to paint, to draw
26**	huàr	画儿	n	painting, drawing, picture
26**	jìn lái	进来	v-comb	to come in, to enter
26**	shīgē	诗歌	n	poem
26**	wǎnfàn	晚饭	n	supper, dinner
26**	xiǎoshuō	小说	n	novel
27	cài	菜	n	dish, vegetable
27	cānzàn	参赞	n	counselor
27	cháng	当	v-act	to taste
27	dàjiā	大家	pron	all, everybody
27	dàshǐ	大使	n	ambassador
27	dàshǐguǎn	大使馆	n	embassy
27	dào	到	v-act	to go, to arrive, to reach
27	fūren	夫人	n	lady, madame, Mrs.
27	gān bēi	干杯	idiom	to propose a toast, here's to...
27	jiànkāng	健康	n, adj, v-st	health, healthy, to be healthy
27	jiǔ	酒	n	wine

Lesson	Pinyin	Characters	Function	English meaning
27	kāishǐ	开始	v-act	to begin, to start
27	kuàizi	筷子	n	chopsticks
27	lóu	楼	n	storied building, floor
27	máotáijiǔ	茅台酒	n	Maotai (a Chinese strong liquor)
27	pútao	葡萄	n	grape
27	pútaojiǔ	葡萄酒	n	grape wine
27	shì	试	v-act	to try
27	wèi	为	prep	for, to
27	wénhuà	文化	n	culture
27	yǒuyì	友谊	n	friendship
27	yòu	又	adv	again, in addition to, more
27	zhāodàihuì	招待会	n	reception
27*	Lǐ	李	n-prop	Li
27**	bìng	病	n, ajd, v-st	illness, disease, sick, to fall ill
27**	báilándì	白兰地	n	brandy
27**	wǔguān	武官	n	military attaché
27**	xiāngbīnjiǔ	香槟酒	n	champagne
27**	xiǎoxuéshēng	小学生	n	pupil, schoolboy/girl
27**	yīmì	一秘	n	first secretary
28	bàn	办	v-act	to handle, to attend, to do
28	bǐ	比	prep, v-act	comparing to..., than, to compare
28	bīngxié	冰鞋	n	skating boots, skates
28	cáipàn	裁判	n, v-act	referee, umpire, to act as a referee
28	dǐng	顶	m	measure word for hat
28	dōngtiān	冬天	n	winter
28	duì	队	n	team
28	gōngping	公平	adj	fair
28	huá bīng	滑冰	v-comb	to skate, skating
28	màozi	帽子	n	hat, cap
28	qì rén	气人	idiom	to get someone angry/annoyed
28	qiānzhèng	签证	n	visa

Lesson	Pinyin	Characters	Function	English meaning
28	qiú	球	n	ball
28	sài	赛	n, v-act	competition, match, to compete
28	shū	输	v-act	to lose
28	shuāng	双	m	pair
28	tī	踢	v-act	to kick
28	wǔfàn	午饭	n	lunch
28	xiāngzi	箱子	n	suitcase
28	xié	鞋	n	shoes
28	xíngli	行李	n	luggage, baggage
28	yíng	赢	v-act	to beat, to win
28	zǎofàn	早饭	n	breakfast
28	zúqiú	足球	n	football
28	zuótiān	昨天	n	yesterday
28**	gōngyuán	公园	n	park
28**	huá xuě	滑雪	v-comb	to ski, skiing
28**	lánqiú	篮球	n	basketball
28**	páiqiú	排球	n	volleyball
28**	pīngpāngqiú	乒乓球	n	table tennis
28**	tǐyùchǎng	体育场	n	stadium
28**	yùndòng	运动	n, v-act	sports, to exercise, to work out
28**	wǎngqiú	网球	n	tennis
29	fàng xīn	放心	idiom	to set one's mind at rest
29	fēijī	飞机	n	aeroplane, plane, aircraft
29	fēnbié	分别	v-act	to part
29	jīchǎng	机场	n	airfield, airport
29	jiàn	见	v-act	to meet, to see
29	jiàn miàn	见面	v-comb	to meet (to see) each other
29	jǐn	紧	adj	close, tight, taut
29	jìnbù	进步	n, v-act	(to) advance, (to)progress
29	líkāi	离开	v-act	to leave
29	míngnián	明年	n	next year

171

Lesson	Pinyin	Characters	Function	English meaning
29	nánguò	难过	adj	sad
29	nǔlì	努力	adj	hard-working, studious
29	qǐfēi	起飞	v-act	to take off
29	qiūtiān	秋天	n	autumn
29	shàng	上	v-act	to get on, to get into, to board
29	shēntǐ	身体	n	body, health
29	suǒyǐ	所以	conj	so, therefore, as a result
29	wàng	忘	v-act	to forget
29	xiàtiān	夏天	n	summer
29	yào	要	adv	will, to be going to
29	yílùpíng'ān	一路平安	idiom	to have a pleasant journey
29	yuànyì	愿意	v-int	to be willing
29	zhàn	站	v-act	to stand
29	zhào xiàng	照像(相)	v-comb	to take a picture
29	zhùyì	注意	v-act	to pay attention to
29**	chuán	船	n	ship
29**	jiào	叫	v-act	to hire, to call (a taxi, etc.)
29**	qìchē	汽车	n	car, vehicle
29**	sòngxíng	送行	v-act	to see someone off
29**	lǚxíng	旅行	v-act	to travel, to tour
29**	Zhōngguó Mínháng	中国民航	n-prop	CAAC
30	dōngxi	东西	n	thing
30	guójiā	国家	n	country
30	guò	过	v-act	to live, to get along
30	kū	哭	v	to cry, to weep
30	lí	离	prep	from
30	nǚ ér	女儿	n	daughter
30	qùnián	去年	n	last year
30	rèqíng	热情	adj	cordial, enthusiastic
30	sòng (rén)	送(人)	v-act	to see (someone) off

Lesson	Pinyin	Characters	Function	English meaning
30	xiào	笑	v-act	to laugh, to smile
30	xīn	心	n	heart
30	yuǎn	远	adj	far, distant
30	zìjǐ	自己	pron	self

PCR I Vocabulary

Pinyin Sequence

Pinyin	Characters	Functions	English meaning	Lesson
a	啊	particle	(a modal particle)	17
à	啊	interj	oh	13
àiren	爱人	n	spouse	14
Ānnà	安娜	n-prop	Anna	24*
ba	吧	particle	(a modal particle)	21
bā	八	number	eight	11
bǎ	把	measure	(a measure word)	22**
bàba	爸爸	n	father	4
bái	白	adj, v-state	white, to be write	16
báilándì	白兰地	n	brandy	27**
bān	班	n	class, squad	15**, 20
bàn	办	v-act	to handle, to attend, to do	28
bàn	半	number	half	17
bāng	帮	v-act	to help	22
bāngzhu	帮助	n, v-act	help, to help	22
bào	报	n	newspaper	5**, 15
bēi	杯	measure	cup	19
Běijīng	北京	n-prop	Beijing	7*, 18*
běn	本	measure	volume	15
běnzi	本子	n	note-book	11**,13**
bǐ	比	prep, v-act	than, to compare	28

Note: The Pinyin list follows the [character/syllable unit + tone number] sequence.

174

Pinyin	Characters	Functions	English meaning	Lesson
bǐ	笔	n	pen, pencil, brush-pen	5**, 13
bǐjiào	比较	adv, v-act	comparatively, to compare	25**
biǎo	表	n	watch	17**
bié	别	adv	don't	19
bīngxié	冰鞋	n	skating boots, skates	28
bìng	病	n, v-state	illness, disease, to fall ill	27**
búcuò	不错	adj	correct, not bad, pretty good	25
bù	不	adv	not, no	3
bù gǎndāng	不敢当	idiom	I don't really deserve it.	15
Bùlǎng	布朗	n-prop	Brown	21*
cáipàn	裁判	n, v-act	referee, to act as a referee	28
cài	菜	n	dish, vegetable	25**, 27
cānguān	参观	v-act	to visit, to pay a visit	23
cānjiā	参加	v-act	to take part in, to attend	20
cāntīng	餐厅	n	dining-hall	22
cānzàn	参赞	n	counsellor	27
cèsuǒ	厕所	n	toilet, lavatory	10**
céng	层	measure	story (of a building)	10
chá	茶	n	tea	8
chà	差	v-state	to be short of, to lack	17
cháng	尝	v-act	to taste	27
cháng	常	adv	often	12
Chángjiāng	长	n-prop	The Yangtze River	7*
chàng	唱	v-act	to sing	19
chàngpiàn	唱片	n	gramophone record	19**
Cháoxiǎn	朝鲜	n-prop	Korea	9**
chē	车	n	car	5
chènshān	衬衫	n	shirt, blouse	16
chéng	城	n	city, town	23
chéngyǔ	成语	n	proverb, idiom	26

Pinyin	Characters	Functions	English meaning	Lesson
chī	吃	v-act	to eat	18
chǐ	尺	n	ruler	5**
chū fā	出发	v-act	to start out, to set off	23
chú fáng	厨房	n	kitchen	22
chuān	穿	v-act	to put on, to wear	16
chuán	船	n	ship	29**
chuāng hu	窗户	n	window	22**
chuáng	床	n	bed	18
cí	词	n	word	24
cí diǎn	词典	n	dictionary	11
cóng	从	co-v	from	16
kā fēi guǎn	咖啡馆	n	cafe	17
dǎ cuò le	打错了	idiom	to have dialled the wrong #	23**
dǎ diànhuà	打电话	v-act	to make a telephone call	23
dà	大	adj, v-state	big, large, to be big	16
dà jiā	大家	pron	all, everybody	27
dà shǐ	大使	n	ambassador	27
dà shǐ guǎn	大使馆	n	embassy	27
Dà yáng Zhōu	大洋洲	n-prop	Oceanaria	7**
dà yī	大衣	n	overcoat, topcoat	16**
dài biǎo	代表	n	delegate, representative	23
dài biǎo tuán	代表团	n	delegation	23
dài fu	大夫	n	doctor	5
dāng	当	v-id	to act as, to serve as	26
dào	到	v-act	to go, to arrive, to reach	27
de	的	particle	(a structural particle)	5
de	得	particle	(a structural particle)	25
Dé guó	德国	n-prop	Germany	6**
děng	等	v-act	to wait	17
dì di	弟弟	n	younger brother	3

176

Pinyin	Characters	Functions	English meaning	Lesson
dì tú	地图	n	map, atlas	7
dì zhǐ	地址	n	address	20
diǎn	点	measure	o'clock, point	17
diǎn xin	点心	n	light refreshments, pastry	24
diàn huà	电话	n	telephone, telephone call	11**, 23
diàn shì	电视	n	television	23
diàn yǐng	电影	n	film, movie	17
diàn yǐng yuàn	电影院	n	cinema	17**
diào	钓	v-act	to fish with a hook and bait	25
Dīng Yún	丁云	n-prop	Ding Yun	9*, 13*
dǐng	顶	measure	(measure word for hat)	28
dōng tiān	冬天	n	winter	28
dōng xi	东西	n	thing	30
dǒng	懂	v-cog	to understand	24
dōu	都	adv	all	3
duàn liàn	锻炼	v-act	to do physical training	24
duì	队	n	team	28
duì	对	v-state	to be right, to be correct	13
duì bu qǐ	对不起	idiom	I'm sorry	20**
duì miàn	对面	n	opposite	22
duō	多	adj, v-st, adv	many, much, a lot of, how	18, 21
duō shao	多少	pron	how many, how much	10
ér zi	儿子	n	son	21**
èr	二	number	two	10
Fǎ guó	法国	n-prop	France	6**, 13**
Fǎ yǔ	法语	n	French	12
fān yì	翻译	n, v-act	interpreter, to interpret	26
fàn	饭	n	meal, cooked rice, food	18
fáng jiān	房间	n	room	22
fáng zi	房子	n	house	22

Pinyin	Characters	Functions	English meaning	Lesson
fǎng wèn	访问	v-act	to visit, to call on	23
fàng xīn	放心	idiom	to set one's mind at rest	29
fēi cháng	非常	adv	extremely	21
fēi jī	飞机	n	aeroplane, plane, aircraft	29
Fēi Zhōu	非洲	n-prop	Africa	7**
fēn	分	measure	minute	17
fēn bié	分别	v-act	to part	29
fēn jī	分机	n	extension	23**
fū ren	夫人	n	lady, madame, Mrs.	27
fú wùyuán	服务员	n	waiter, waitress, attendant	19
fǔ dǎo	辅导	v-act	to coach	20
fù xí	复习	v-act	to review	23
gān bēi	干杯	idiom	to propose a toast, here's to...	27
gān jìng	干净	adj, v-state	clean, neat, to be clean	21**
gǎn xiè	感谢	v-act	to thank	21
gāo xìng	高兴	adj, v-state	happy, to be delighted	21
gào su	告诉	v-act	to tell	14
gē-r	歌儿	n	song	19
gē ge	哥哥	n	elder brother	3
gē jù	歌剧	n	opera	26**
ge	个	measure	a measure word	15
gěi	给	co-v, v-act	for, to, to give	14
gēn	跟	co-v, v-act	with, to follow	17
gèng	更	adv	even, still	21
gōng chǎng	工厂	n	factory	23
gōng chéng shī	工程师	n	engineer	14**
gōng ping	公平	adj	fair	28
gōng rén	工人	n	worker	23
gōng sī	公司	n	company	14**
gōng yuán	公园	n	park	28**

Pinyin	Characters	Functions	English meaning	Lesson
gōng zuò	工作	n, v	work, to work	14
gū niang	姑娘	n	girl	21
Gǔ bō	古波	n-prop	Gubo	1*, 13*
gǔ diǎn	古典	n	classical, classic	19
guì xìng	贵姓	idiom	What's your name?	9
Guō Mòruò	郭沫若	n-prop	Guo Moruo	26*
guó	国	n	country, state	6
guó jiā	国家	n	country	30
guò	过	v-act	to live, to get along	30
hái	还	adv	still, in addition, else	15
hái shì	还是	conj	or	19
hái zi	孩子	n	child	14
Hàn yǔ	汉语	n	Chinese (language)	6
Hàn zì	汉字	n	Chinese character	15
hǎo	好	adj, v-state	good, to be good, to be well	1
hǎo kàn	好看	adj, v-state	good-looking, to be beautiful	21
hào	号	n	number, date, day of the month	10, 20
hào mǎ	号码	n	number	23**
hē	喝	v-act	to drink	8
hé	河	n	river	25
hé	和	conj	and, with	13
hēi	黑	adj, v-state	black, to be black	16**
hěn	很	adv	very	2
hóng	红	adj, v-state	red, to be red	19
hóng chá	红茶	n	black tea	19
hòu biān	后边	n	back, at the back of, behind	22
hù xiāng	互相	adv	each other, mutually	15
huā chá	花茶	n	scented tea, jasmine tea	19
huā r	花儿	n	flower	21
huā yuán	花园	n	garden	22

179

Pinyin	Characters	Functions	English meaning	Lesson
huá bīng	滑冰	v-comb	to skate, skating	28
huá xuě	滑雪	v-comb	to ski, skiing	28**
huà	画	v-act	to paint, to draw	26**
huà bào	画报	n	pictorial	11
huà-r	画儿	n	painting, drawing, picture	26**
huān yíng	欢迎	v-act	to welcome	8
huán	还	v-act	to return	11
Huáng Hé	黄河	n-prop	The Yellow River	7*
huí	回	v-act	to return	17
huí dá	回答	v-act	to reply, to answer	24
huì	会	aux v	to know how to, can	26
huǒ chē	火车	n	train	24
huǒ tuǐ	火腿	n	ham	25
huò zhě	或者	conj	or	26
jī chǎng	机场	n	airfield, airport	29
jī dàn	鸡蛋	n	hen's egg	25**
jǐ	几	number, pron	several, how many, how much	15
jiā	家	n	family, home, house	14
jiā shēn	加深	v-act	to deepen	26
jiàn	见	v-act	to meet, to see	29
jiàn	件	measure	a measure word	16
jiàn kāng	健	adj, n, v-state	healthy, health, to be healthy	27
jiàn miàn	见面	v-comb	to meet (to see) each other	29
jiāo	教	v-act	to teach	15
jiǎo zi	饺子	n	Chinese dumpling	25**
jiào	叫	v-id, v-act	to be called, to hire, to call	9, 29**
jiào liàn	教练	n	coach, trainer	25
jiào shì	教室	n	classroom	15**
jiào shòu	教授	n	professor	13**
jiē diàn huà	接电话	v-act	to answer a phone	23

Pinyin	Characters	Functions	English meaning	Lesson
jiē (rén)	接(人)	v-act	to meet one at a station/airport	23
jié hūn	结婚	v-comb	to get married	20**
jiě jie	姐姐	n	elder sister	14
jiè	借	v-act	to borrow, to lend	15**
jiè shào	介绍	v-act	to introduce	13
jīn nián	今年	n	this year	20
jīn tiān	今天	n	today	20
jǐn	紧	adj	close, tight, taut	29
jìn	进	v-act	to enter, to come in	8
jìn bù	进步	n, v-act	progress, to make progress	29
jìn lái	进来	v-comb	to come in, to enter	26**
jīng jù	京剧	n	Beijing opera	16
jīng lǐ	经理	n	manager, director	14**
jiǔ	酒	n	wine	27
jiǔ	九	number	nine	11
jiù	就	adv, conj	at once, right away	26
jiù	旧	adj, v-state	old, to be old	16
jú zi	桔子	n	orange	19
jú zi shuǐ	桔子水	n	orangeade, orange juice	19
jù chǎng	剧场	n	theatre	16**
kā fēi	咖啡	n	coffee	8**, 17
kāi	开	v-act	to open	21
kāi (chē)	开(车)	v-act	to drive (a car)	23
kāi shǐ	开始	v-act	to begin, to start	27
kàn	看	v-act	to look, to read, to watch	7
kě shì	可是	conj	but	26
kě yǐ	可以	aux v	may	26
kè	刻	measure	quarter (or an hour)	17
kè	课	n	class	17
kè qi	客气	adj, v-state	polite, to be polite	8

N the Location + Shi +ig!!

S + zai + Location de+N

Pinyin	Characters	Functions	English meaning	Lesson
kè tīng	客厅	n	drawing room, parlour	22
kè wén	课文	n	text	23
kòng-r	空儿	n	spare time	20
kǒu yǔ	口语	n	spoken language	15
kū	哭	v-act	to cry, to weep	30
kù zi	裤子	n	trousers	16**
kuài	快	adj	fast, quick	25
kuài zi	筷子	n	chopsticks	27
kuàng quán shuǐ	矿泉水	n	mineral water	25
lái	来	v-act	to come	13
lán	蓝	adj, v-state	blue, to be blue	16**
lán qiú	篮球	n	basketball	28**
lǎo	老	adj., v-state	old, to be old	6
lǎo shī	老师	n	teacher	6
le	了	particle	(a modal particle)	13
lí	离	prep	from	30
lí kāi	离开	v-act	to leave	29
Lǐ	李	n-prop	Li	27*
lǐ biān	里边	n	inside	22
lǐ wù	礼物	n	present, gift	21**
lǐ xiǎng	理想	n, adj	ideal	26
liǎ	俩	m	both, two	26
liàn xí	练习	n, v-act	exercise, to practice	24
liǎng	两	number	two	16
liàng	辆	measure	measure word for vehicle	21**
liǎo jiě	了解	v-cog	to understand, to know	26
líng	零	number	zero	10
liú lì	流利	adj	fluent	25**
liú xué shēng	留学生	n	a foreign student	9
liù	六	number	six	11

182

Pinyin	Characters	Functions	English meaning	Lesson
lóu	楼	n	storied building, floor	27
Lǔ Xùn	鲁迅	n-prop	Lu Xun	26*
lù	路	n	road, way	17
lǜ	绿	adj, v-state	green, to be green	16
lǜ chá	绿茶	n	green tea	19**
ma	吗	particle	(an interrogative particle)	2
māma	妈妈	n	mother	4
Mǎ lǐ	马里	n-prop	Mali	6**
mǎi	买	v-act	to buy	13
màn	慢	adj	slow	25
máng	忙	adj, v-state	busy, to be busy	3
máo táijiǔ	茅台酒	n	Maotai (a Chinese liquor)	27
mào zi	帽子	n	hat, cap	28
méi	没	adv, v-poss	not, no, do not have	14
méi guān xi	没关系	idiom	it doesn't matter	20**
méi (you)	没(有)	adv	not, no	23
měi	每	pron	every, each	18
Měi guó	美国	n-prop	U.S.A.	6**
mèi mei	妹妹	n	younger sister	14
mén	门	n	door	21
miàn bāo	面包	n	bread	25
mín gē	民歌	n	folk song	19
míng nián	明年	n	next year	20**, 29
míng tiān	明天	n	tomorrow	23
míng zi	名字	n	name	13
nǎ	哪	pron	which	6
nǎr	哪儿	pron	where	10
nǎ li	哪里	idiom	it is nothing	25
nà	那	pron	that	5
nà-r	那儿	pron	there	10**, 15

Pinyin	Characters	Functions	English meaning	Lesson
nǎi lào	奶酪	n	cheese	25
nán	难	adj, v-state	difficult, to be difficult	24
nán	男	adj	male	13
nán guò	难过	adj	sad	29
Nán Měi Zhōu	南美洲	n-prop	South America	7**
ne	呢	particle	(a modal particle)	2
néng	能	aux v	can, to be able to	26
nǐ	你	pron	you	1
nǐ men	你们	pron	you (pl.)	4
nián	年	n	year	20
nián qīng	年轻	adj, v-state	young, to be young	21
niàn	念	v-act	to read (aloud), to study	24
nín	您	pron	you (polite form of "nǐ")	8
niú nǎi	牛奶	n	(cows) milk	8**, 25**
nóng cūn	农村	n	countryside, rural areas	24
nóng mín	农民	n	peasant	24
nǔ lì	努力	adj	hard-working, studious	29
nǚ	女	adj	female	12
nǚ ér	女儿	n	daughter	21**, 30
nǚ shì	女士	n	polite address to a lady	9**
Ōu Zhōu	欧洲	n-prop	Europe	7**
Pà lán kǎ	帕兰卡	n-prop	Palanka	1*, 13**
pái qiú	排球	n	volleyball	28**
páng biān	旁边	n	side	22
péng you	朋友	n	friend	4
pí jiǔ	啤酒	n	beer	8**, 19
piào	票	n	ticket	16
piào liang	漂亮	adj, v-state	pretty, beautiful, to be pretty	21
pīng pāng qiú	乒乓球	n	table tennis	28**
píng	瓶	measure	bottle	19

Pinyin	Characters	Functions	English meaning	Lesson
píng guǒ	苹果	n	apple	19**
pú tao	葡萄	n	grape	19**, 27
pú tao jiǔ	葡萄酒	n	grape wine	27
qī	七	number	seven	11
qǐ	起	v-act	to get up, to rise	18
qǐ chuáng	起床	idiom	to get up	18
qǐ fēi	起飞	v-act	to take off	29
qì chē	汽车	n	car, vehicle	29**
qì rén	气人	idiom	to get someone angry/annoyed	28
qiān zhèng	签证	n	visa	28
qián biān	前边	n	front, in front of, before	22**, 25
qīng chu	清楚	adj	clear, distinct	25**
qǐng	请	v-act	please	8
qǐng wèn	请问	idiom	May I ask...?	9
qiū tiān	秋天	n	autumn	29
qiú	球	n	ball	28
qù	去	v-act	to go	12
qù nián	去年	n	last year	20**, 30
qún zi	裙子	n	skirt	16
ràng	让	v-act	to let, to ask	19
rè qíng	热情	adj	cordial, enthusiastic	30
rén	人	n	person	6
rén mín	人民	n	people	26
Rén mín Rì bào	人民日报	n-prop	The People's Daily	23*
rèn shi	认识	v-cog	to know, to recognize	12
rèn zhēn	认真	adj, v-state	conscientious, (to be) serious	24
rì	日	n	date, day of the month	20
Rì běn	日本	n-prop	Japan	6**, 21*
róng yi	容易	adj	easy	26
sài	赛	n, v-act	competition, match, to compete	28

Pinyin	Characters	Functions	English meaning	Lesson
sān	三	number	three	10
shāng diàn	商店	n	shop	13
shàng	上	v-act	to get on, to get into, to board	29
shàng bān	上班	idiom	to go to work	17**
shàng biān	上边	n	top, on, over, above	22
Shàng hǎi	上海	n-prop	Shanghai	7*
shàng (kè)	上课	v-act	to attend or to teach (a class)	17
shàng wǔ	上午	n	morning	18
shàng yī	上衣	n	upper outer garment	16**
shǎo	少	adj, v-state	few, little, to be few	22
Cháng chéng	长城	n-prop	The Great Wall	7*
shei	谁	pron	who	6
shēn tǐ	身体	n	body, health	29
shén me	什么	pron	what	7
shēng cí	生词	n	new word	15**, 24
shēng ri	生日	n	birthday	20
shī gē	诗歌	n	poem	26**
shí	十	number	ten	11
shí táng	食堂	n	dining-hall	17
shí yànshì	实验室	n	laboratory	15**
shì	试	v-act	to try	27
shì	是	v-id	to be	4
shì-r	事儿	n	business, thing	17
shì jiè	世界	n	world	7**
shū	书	n	book	5
shū	输	v-act	to lose	28
shū diàn	书店	n	bookstore	14
shū fáng	书房	n	study	22
shù	束	measure	bunch	21
shuāng	双	measure	pair	28

186

Pinyin	Characters	Functions	English meaning	Lesson
shuǐ	水	n	water	19
shuì jiào	睡觉	idiom	to go to bed, to sleep	18
shuō	说	v-act	to speak, to say	13
sì	四	number	four	10
sòng	送	v-act	to give, to give as a present	21
sòng (rén)	送 (人)	v(-comb)-act	to see (someone) off	30
sòng xíng	送行	v-act	to see someone off	29**
sù shè	宿舍	n	dormitory	10
suì	岁	measure	year (age)	20
suì shu	岁数	n	age	21**
suǒ yǐ	所以	conj	so, therefore, as a result	29
tā	他	pron	he, him	3
tā	她	pron	she, her	5
tāmen	他们	pron	they, them	3
tāmen	她们	pron	they, them (for females)	12
tài	太	adv	too, too much	16
tài tai	太太	n	Mrs., madame	8**, 21
tán	谈	v-act	to talk, to chat	20**, 26
tāng	汤	n	soup	25
táng	糖	n	sugar, sweets, candy	19**
tào	套	measure	set	22**
tī	踢	v-act	to kick	28
tǐ yù chǎng	体育场	n	stadium	28**
tiān	天	n	day	18
tiáo	条	measure	a measure word	16
tiào wǔ	跳舞	v-comb	to dance	21
tīng	听	v-act	to listen	19
tíng	停	v-act	to stop, to come to a stop	25
tóng xué	同学	n	classmate, schoolmate	20
tóng zhì	同志	n	comrade	9**

Pinyin	Characters	Functions	English meaning	Lesson
tú shū guǎn	图书馆	n	library	15
yùn dòng	运动	v-act	to exercise, to work out	28**
wài biān	外边	n	outside	22**, 23
wài yǔ	外语	n	foreign language	9
wán-r	玩儿	v-act	to play, to have fun with	23
wǎn	晚	adj	late	25
wǎn fàn	晚饭	n	supper, dinner	26**
wǎn shang	晚上	n	evening	16
Wáng	王	n-prop	Wang	8*, 15*
Wáng Shūwén	王书文	n-prop	Wang Shuwen	24*
wǎng qiú	网球	n	tennis	28**
wàng	忘	v-act	to forget	29
wèi	位	measure	measure word	25
wèi	为	prep	for, to	27
wèi	喂	interj	hello	13
wén huà	文化	n	culture	27
wén xué	文学	n	literature	26
wèn	问	v-act	to ask	9
wèn tí	问题	n	question	18
wǒ	我	pron	I, me	2
wǒ men	我们	pron	we, us	6
wò shì	卧室	n	bedroom	22
wǔ	五	number	five	10
wǔ fàn	午饭	n	lunch	28
wǔ guān	武官	n	military attaché	27**
wǔ huì	舞会	n	dance, ball	20
xī yān	吸煙(烟)	v-act	to smoke	8
xǐ huan	喜欢	v-act	to like, to be fond of	19
xǐ zǎo	洗澡	v-act	to take a bath	22
xǐ zǎo jiān	洗澡间	n	bathroom	22

Pinyin	Characters	Functions	English meaning	Lesson
xì	系	n	department, faculty	15
xià bān	下班	idiom	to come or go off work	17**
xià biān	下边	n	bottom	22**
xià (kè)	下课	v-act	class is over or dismissed	17
xià tiān	夏天	n	summer	29
xià wǔ	下午	n	afternoon	18
xiān sheng	先生	n	Mr., sir, gentleman	8**, 12
xiàn dài	现代	n	modern	19
xiàn zài	现在	n	now, nowadays	11
xiāng bīn jiǔ	香槟酒	n	champagne	27**
xiāng jiāo	香蕉	n	banana	19**
xiāng zi	箱子	n	suitcase	28
xiǎng	想	v-act, v-int	to miss, to think, to want	14
xiang	象	v-id	to be like, to resemble	21
xiǎo	小	adj, v-state	little, small, to be small	22
xiǎo jie	小姐	n	miss, young lady	9**, 19
xiǎo shuō	小说	n	novel	26**
xiǎo xué shēng	小学生	n	pupil, schoolboy/girl	27**
xiào	笑	v-act	to laugh, to smile	30
xiē	些	measure	some	24
xié	鞋	n	shoes	28
xiě	写	v-act	to write	14
xiè xie	谢谢	v-act	to thank	8
xīn	心	n	heart	30
xīn	新	adj, v-state	new, to be new	15
xīn nián	新年	n	New Year	21**
xīn wén	新闻	n	news	23
xìn	信	n	letter	14
xīng qī	星期	n	week	20
xīng qī rì	星期日	n	Sunday	20

Pinyin	Characters	Functions	English meaning	Lesson
xíng li	行李	n	luggage, baggage	28
xìng	姓	n, v-id	a surname, (one's) surname is	9
xiū xi	休息	v-act	to take a rest	18
xué	学	v-act	to study, to learn	9
xué sheng	学生	n	student	9
xué xí	学习	v-act	to study, to learn	9
xué yuàn	学院	n	college, institute	9
lǚ xíng	旅行	v-act	to travel, to tour	29**
yān	煙(烟)	n	cigarette, smoke	8
yán jiu	研究	n, v-act	research, to research, to study	26
yào	要	v-act, v-int	to want; must, to be going to	19
yào	要	aux v	will, to be going to	29
yě	也	adv	also, too	2
yī	一	number	one	10
yī mì	一秘	n	first secretary	27**
yī yuàn	医院	n	hospital	10**
yí dìng	一定	adj, adv	particular, surely, certainly	20
yí lù píng ān	一路平安	idiom	to have a pleasant journey	29
yí xiàr	一下儿	idiom	a little while	11
yǐ hòu	以后	n	later on, in the future	17
yǐ qián	以前	n	before, in the past, ago	17**
yǐ zi	椅子	n	chair	22
yì diǎnr	一点儿	idiom	a little, a bit	25
yì qǐ	一起	adv	together	17
yīn yuè	音乐	n	music	19
yīn yuè huì	音乐会	n	concert	20**
yín háng	银行	n	bank	14
yīng gāi	应该	aux v	should, ought to	26
Yīng guó	英国	n-prop	Britain	9**, 13**
Yīng yǔ	英语	n	English	12

190

Pinyin	Characters	Functions	English meaning	Lesson
yíng	赢	v-act	to beat, to win	28
yòng	用	v-act	to use, to make use of	11
yóu jú	邮局	n	post office	13**
yóu piào	邮票	n	stamp	13**
yóu yǒng	游泳	v-comb	to swim, swimming	25
yǒu	有	v-poss	to have, there be	14
yǒu hǎo	友好	adj, v-state	friendly, to be friendly	23
yǒu míng	有名	adj	famous, well-known	26
yǒu shí hou	有时候	idiom	sometimes	18
yǒu yì	友谊	n	friendship	27
yǒu yì si	有意思	idiom	interesting	20
yòu	又	adv	again, in addition to, more	27
yòu biān	右边	n	right	22**
yú	鱼	n	fish	25
yǔ fǎ	语法	n	grammar	15
yǔ sǎn	雨伞	n	umbrella	11**
yuǎn	远	adj	far, distant	30
yuàn yì	愿意	v-int	to be willing	29
yuē huì	约会	n	appointment	20**
yuè	月	n	month	20
yuè lǎn shì	阅览室	n	reading room	15
yùn dòng	运动	n	sports	28**
zá zhì	杂志	n	magazine	11**, 15
zài	再	adv	again, once more	25
zài	在	v-loc	to be at, to be in	10
zài jiàn	再见	idiom	See you again; Good bye	11
zǎo	早	adj	early	26
zǎo fàn	早饭	n	breakfast	28
zěn me yàng	怎么样	idiom	how is it	22
zhàn	站	v-act	to stand	29

191

Pinyin	Characters	Functions	English meaning	Lesson
zhàn xiàn	占线	idiom	the line is busy	23**
zhāng	张	measure	piece	16
zhāo dài huì	招待会	n	reception	27
zhǎo	找	v-act	to look for, to call on (a person)	16
zhào piàn	照片	n	photograph, picture	21**, 23
zhào xiàng	照像(相)	v-comb	to take a picture	29
zhè	这	pron	this	4
zhè-r	这儿	pron	here	10**, 16
zhēn	真	adj	real, true, genuine	21
zhěng lǐ	整理	v-act	to put in order, to straighten up	22
zhěng qí	整齐	adj, v-state	tidy, to be tidy	25**
zhèng zài	正在	adv	(action in progress)	23
zhī	枝	measure	branch, etc.	19**
zhī dao	知道	v-cog	to know	20
zhí yuán	职员	n	office worker, staff	14**
zhǐ	纸	n	paper	5**, 13
zhōng	钟	n	clock	17**
Zhōng guó	中国	n-prop	China	6*, 13*
Zhōngguó Mínháng	中国民航	n-prop	CAAC	29**
zhōng jiān	中间	n	middle	22**
Zhōng wén	中文	n	Chinese (language)	15
zhù	祝	v-act	to wish	21
zhù	住	v-loc	to live	10
zhù hè	祝贺	n, v-act	congratulation, to congratulate	20
zhù yì	注意	v-act	to pay attention to	29
zhǔn bèi	准备	v-act	to prepare	25
zhuō zi	桌子	n	table	22
zì	字	n	character	15
zì jǐ	自己	pron	self	30
zǒng	总	adv	always	22

Pinyin	Characters	Functions	English meaning	Lesson
zǒng jī	总机	n	central exchange, switchboard	23**
zǒng shì	总是	adv	always	22
zǒu	走	v-act	to go, to walk	17
zú qiú	足球	n	football	28
zuó tiān	昨天	n	yesterday	28
zuǒ biān	左边	n	left	22
zuò	坐	v-act	to sit, to take a seat	10
zuò	作	v-act	to do	14
zuòjiā	作家	n	writer	26
zuòwèi	座位	n	seat	16**

PCR I Vocabulary

English Sequence

English meaning	Pinyin	Characters	Functions	Lesson
a little	yì diǎnr	一点儿	idiom	25
a little while	yíxiàr	一下儿	idiom	11
above	shàngbiān	上边	n	22
across from	duì miàn	对面	n	22
address	dì zhǐ	地址	n	20
advance	jì nbù	进步	n	29
aeroplane	fēij ī	飞机	n	29
Africa	Fēi Zhōu	非洲	n-prop	7**
afternoon	xiàwǔ	下午	n	18
again	yòu	又	adv	27
again	zài	再	adv	25
age	suì shu	岁数	n	21**
ago	yǐqián	以前	n	17**
aircraft, airplane	fēij ī	飞机	n	29
airport	jīchǎng	机场	n	29
all	dōu	都	adv	3
all	dàjiā	大家	pron	27
also	yě	也	adv	2
always	zǒng(shì)	总(是)	adv	22
ambassador	dàshǐ	大使	n	27
America	Měiguó	美国	n-prop	6**
and	hé	和	conj	13
Anna	Ānnà	安娜	n-prop	24*

English meaning	Pinyin	Characters	Functions	Lesson
apple	píngguǒ	苹果	n	19**
appointment	yuēhuì	约会	n	20**
as a result	suǒyǐ	所以	conj	29
at once	jiù	就	adv	26
atlas	dìtú	地图	n	7
attendant	fúwùyuán	服务员	n	19
autumn	qiūtiān	秋天	n	29
back	hòubiān	后边	n	22
baggage	xíngli	行李	n	28
ball	qiú	球	n	28
ball	wǔhuì	舞会	n	20
banana	xiāngjiāo	香蕉	n	19**
bank	yínháng	银行	n	14
basketball	lánqiú	篮球	n	28**
bathroom	xǐzǎojiān	洗澡间	n	22
beautiful	piàoliang	漂亮	adj	21
bed	chuáng	床	n	18
bedroom	wòshì	卧室	n	22
beer	píjiǔ	啤酒	n	8**, 19
before	yǐqián	以前	n	17**
Beijing	Běijīng	北京	n-prop	7*, 18*
Beijing opera	jīngjù	京剧	n	16
big	dà	大	adj	16
birthday	shēngri	生日	n	20
black	hēi	黑	adj	16**
black tea	hóngchá	红茶	n	19
blouse	chènshān	衬衫	n	16
blue	lán	蓝	adj	16**
body	shēntǐ	身体	n	29
book	shū	书	n	5
bookstore	shūdiàn	书店	n	14

English meaning	Pinyin	Characters	Functions	Lesson
both	liǎ	俩	measure	26
bottle	píng	瓶	measure	19
bottom	xiàbiān	下边	n	22**
branch, etc.	zhī	枝	measure	19**
brandy	báilándì	白兰地	n	27**
bread	miànbāo	面包	n	25
breakfast	zǎofàn	早饭	n	28
Britain	Yīngguó	英国	n-prop	9**, 13**
Brown	Bùlǎng	布朗	n-prop	21*
brush-pen	bǐ	笔	n	5**, 13
bunch	shù	束	measure	21
business	shìr	事儿	n	17
busy	máng	忙	adj	3
but	kěshì	可是	conj	26
CAAC	Zhōngguó Mínháng	中国民航	n-prop	29**
café	kāfēiguǎn	咖啡馆	n	17
can	huì	会	aux v	26
candy	táng	糖	n	19**
cap	màozi	帽子	n	28
car	chē	车	n	5
car	qìchē	汽车	n	29**
central exchange	zǒngjī	总机	n	23**
certainly	yídìng	一定	adv	20
chair	yǐzi	椅子	n	22
champagne	xiāngbīnjiǔ	香槟酒	n	27**
character	zì	字	n	15
cheese	nǎilào	奶酪	n	25
child	háizi	孩子	n	14
China	Zhōngguó	中国	n-prop	6*, 13*
Chinese (language)	Zhōngwén	中文	n	15
Chinese (oral language)	Hànyǔ	汉语	n	6

English meaning	Pinyin	Characters	Functions	Lesson
Chinese character	Hànzì	汉字	n	15
Chinese dumpling	jiǎozi	饺子	n	25**
chopsticks	kuàizi	筷子	n	27
cigarette	yān	烟	n	8
cinema	diànyǐngyuàn	电影院	n	17**
city, town	chéng	城	n	23
class	kè	课	n	17
class	bān	班	n	15**, 20
class is over or dismissed	xià(kè)	下课	v-comb	17
classic, classical	gǔdiǎn	古典	n	19
classmate	tóngxué	同学	n	20
classroom	jiàoshì	教室	n	15**
clean	gānjìng	干净	adj	21**
clear	qīngchu	清楚	adj	25**
clock	zhōng	钟	n	17**
close	jǐn	紧	adj	29
coach	jiàoliàn	教练	n	25
coffee	kāfēi	咖啡	n	8**, 17
college	xuéyuàn	学院	n	9
company	gōngsī	公司	n	14**
comparatively	bǐjiào	比较	adv	25**
comparing to...	bǐ	比	prep	28
competition	sài	赛	n	28
comrade	tóngzhì	同志	n	9**
concert	yīnyuèhuì	音乐会	n	20**
congratulation	zhùhè	祝贺	n	20
conscientious	rènzhēn	认真	adj	24
contemporary	xiàndài	现代	n	19
cooked rice	fàn	饭	n	18
cordial	rèqíng	热情	adj	30
correct	búcuò	不错	adj	25

English meaning	Pinyin	Characters	Functions	Lesson
counselor	cānzàn	参赞	n	27
country	guójiā	国家	n	30
country	guó	国	n	6
countryside	nóngcūn	农村	n	24
culture	wénhuà	文化	n	27
cup	bēi	杯	measure	19
dance	wǔhuì	舞会	n	20
dancing party	wǔhuì	舞会	n	20
date	hào, rì	号, 日	n	20
daughter	nǚ ér	女儿	n	21**, 30
day	tiān	天	n	18
day of the month	hào, rì	号, 日	n	20
delegate	dàibiǎo	代表	n	23
delegation	dàibiǎotuán	代表团	n	23
department	xì	系	n	15
dialed the wrong number	dǎ cuò le	打错了	idiom	23**
dictionary	cídiǎn	词典	n	11
difficult	nán	难	adj	24
Ding Yun	Dīng Yún	丁云	n-prop	9*, 13*
dining-hall	cāntīng	餐厅	n	22
dining-hall	shítáng	食堂	n	17
dinner	wǎnfàn	晚饭	n	26**
director	jīnglǐ	经理	n	14**
disease	bìng	病	n	27**
dish	cài	菜	n	25**, 27
distant	yuǎn	远	adj	30
distinct	qīngchu	清楚	adj	25**
do not have	méi	没	v-poss	14
doctor	dàifu	大夫	n	5
don't	bié	别	adv	19

English meaning	Pinyin	Characters	Functions	Lesson
door	mén	门	n	21
dormitory	sùshè	宿舍	n	10
drawing	huàr	画儿	n	26**
drawing room	kètīng	客厅	n	22
each	měi	每	pron	18
each other	hùxiāng	互相	adv	15
early	zǎo	早	adj	26
easy	róngyi	容易	adj	26
eight	bā	八	number	11
elder brother	gēge	哥哥	n	3
elder sister	jiějie	姐姐	n	14
else	hái	还	adv	15
embassy	dàshǐguǎn	大使馆	n	27
engineer	gōngchéngshī	工程师	n	14**
English language	Yīngyǔ	英语	n	12
enthusiastic	rèqíng	热情	adj	30
Europe	Ōu Zhōu	欧洲	n-prop	7**
even, still	gèng	更	adv	21
evening	wǎnshang	晚上	n	16
every	měi	每	pron	18
everybody	dàjiā	大家	pron	27
exchange student	líuxuéshēng	留学生	n	9
excited	gāoxìng	高兴	adj	21
exercise	liànxí	练习	n	24
extension	fēnjī	分机	n	23**
extraordinarily	fēicháng	非常	adv	21
extremely	fēicháng	非常	adv	21
factory	gōngchǎng	工厂	n	23
faculty	xì	系	n	15
fair	gōngping	公平	adj	28
family	jiā	家	n	14

English meaning	Pinyin	Characters	Functions	Lesson
famous	yǒumíng	有名	adj	26
far	yuǎn	远	adj	30
fast	kuài	快	adj	25
father	bàba	爸爸	n	4
female	nǚ	女	adj	12
few	shǎo	少	adj	22
film	diànyǐng	电影	n	17
first secretary	yīmì	一秘	n	27**
fish	yú	鱼	n	25
five	wǔ	五	number	10
floor	lóu	楼	n	27
flower	huār	花儿	n	21
fluent	liúlì	流利	adj	25**
folk song	míngē	民歌	n	19
food	fàn	饭	n	18
football	zúqiú	足球	n	28
for	wèi	为	prep	27
for	gěi	给	co-v	14
foreign language	wàiyǔ	外语	n	9
foreign student	liúxuéshēng	留学生	n	9
four	sì	四	number	10
France	Fǎguó	法国	n-prop	6**, 13**
French	Fǎyǔ	法语	n	12
friend	péngyou	朋友	n	4
friendly	yǒuhǎo	友好	adj	23
friendship	yǒuyì	友谊	n	27
from	cóng	从	co-v	16
from	lí	离	prep	30
front	qiánbiān	前边	n	22**, 25
garden	huāyuán	花园	n	22
gentleman	xiānsheng	先生	n	8**, 12

English meaning	Pinyin	Characters	Functions	Lesson
genuine	zhēn	真	adj	21
Germany	Déguó	德国	n-prop	6**
gift	lǐwù	礼物	n	21**
girl	gūniang	姑娘	n	21
Good bye	zàijiàn	再见	idiom	11
Good morning!	zǎo	早	adj	26
good	hǎo	好	adj	1
good-looking	hǎokàn	好看	adj	21
grammar	yǔfǎ	语法	n	15
gramophone record	chàngpiàn	唱片	n	19**
grape	pútao	葡萄	n	19**, 27
grape wine	pútaojiǔ	葡萄酒	n	27
green	lǜ	绿	adj, v-state	16
green tea	lǜchá	绿茶	n	19**
Gubo	Gǔbō	古波	n-prop	1*, 13*
Guo Moruo	Guō Mòruò	郭沫若	n-prop	26*
half	bàn	半	number	17
ham	huǒtuǐ	火腿	n	25
happy	gāoxìng	高兴	adj	21
hard-working	nǔlì	努力	adj	29
hat	màozi	帽子	n	28
he	tā	他	pron	3
health	shēntǐ	身体	n	29
health	jiànkāng	健康	n	27
healthy	jiànkāng	健康	adj	27
heart	xīn	心	n	30
hello	wèi	喂	interj	13
help	bāngzhu	帮助	n	22
hen's egg	jīdàn	鸡蛋	n	25**
her	tā	她	pron	5

English meaning	Pinyin	Characters	Functions	Lesson
here	zhèr	这儿	pron	10**, 16
here's to...	gān bēi	干杯	idiom	27
him	tā	他	pron	3
home	jiā	家	n	14
hospital	yīyuàn	医院	n	10**
house	jiā	家	n	14
house	fángzi	房子	n	22
how	duō	多	adv	21
how is it	zěnmeyàng	怎么样	idiom	22
how many (much)	duōshao	多少	pron	10
how many, how much	jǐ	几	pron	15
husband	xiānsheng	先生	n	8**, 12
I	wǒ	我	pron	2
I don't really deserve it.	bù gǎndāng	不敢当	idiom	15
I'm sorry	duì bu qǐ	对不起	idiom	20**
ideal	lǐxiǎng	理想	adj, n	26
idiom	chéngyǔ	成语	n	26
illness	bìng	病	n	27**
in addition	hái	还	adv	15
in addition to	yòu	又	adv	27
in the midst of	zhèngzài	正在	adv	23
inside	lǐbiān	里边	n	22
institute	xuéyuàn	学院	n	9
interesting	yǒu yì si	有意思	idiom	20
interpreter	fānyì	翻译	n	26
it doesn't matter	méi guānxi	没关系	idiom	20**
it is nothing	nǎli	哪里	idiom	25
Japan	Rì běn	日本	n-prop	6**, 21*
jasmine tea	huāchá	花茶	n	19
kitchen	chúfáng	厨房	n	22
Korea	Cháoxiǎn	朝鲜	n-prop	9**

English meaning	Pinyin	Characters	Functions	Lesson
laboratory	shíyànshì	实验室	n	15**
lady, Madame, Mrs.	fūren	夫人	n	27
last year	qùnián	去年	n	20**, 30
late	wǎn	晚	adj	25
later on, in the future	yǐhòu	以后	n	17
lavatory	cèsuǒ	厕所	n	10**
left	zuǒbiān	左边	n	22
letter	xìn	信	n	14
Li	Lǐ	李	n-prop	27*
library	túshūguǎn	图书馆	n	15
light refreshments	diǎnxin	点心	n	24
literature	wénxué	文学	n	26
little	shǎo	少	adj	22
little	xiǎo	小	adj	22
living room	kètīng	客厅	n	22
Lu Xun	Lǔ Xùn	鲁迅	n-prop	26*
luggage	xíngli	行李	n	28
lunch	wǔfàn	午饭	n	28
Madame	tàitai	太太	n	8**, 21
magazine	zázhì	杂志	n	11**, 15
male	nán	男	adj	13
Mali	Mǎlǐ	马里	n-prop	6**
manager	jīnglǐ	经理	n	14**
many	duō	多	adv	21
many	duō	多	adj, v-state	18
Maotai (a strong liquor)	máotáijiǔ	茅台酒	n	27
map	dìtú	地图	n	7
match	sài	赛	n	28
May I ask...?	qǐngwèn	请问	idiom	9
may	kěyǐ	可以	aux v	26
me	wǒ	我	pron	2

English meaning	Pinyin	Characters	Functions	Lesson
meal	fàn	饭	n	18
middle	zhōngjiān	中间	n	22**
military attaché	wǔguān	武官	n	27**
milk, (cow's)	niúnǎi	牛奶	n	8**, 25**
mineral water	kuàngquánshuǐ	矿泉水	n	25
minute	fēn	分	measure	17
miss	xiǎojie	小姐	n	9**, 19
modern	xiàndài	现代	n	19
month	yuè	月	n	20
more	yòu	又	adv	27
morning	shàngwǔ	上午	n	18
mother	māma	妈妈	n	4
movie	diànyǐng	电影	n	17
Mr.	xiānsheng	先生	n	8**, 12
Mrs.	tàitai	太太	n	8**, 21
much	duō	多	adj, v-state	18
music	yīnyuè	音乐	n	19
must	yào	要	v-int	19
mutually	hùxiāng	互相	adv	15
name	míngzi	名字	n	13
neat	gānjing	干净	adj	21**
New Year	xīnnián	新年	n	21**
new	xīn	新	adj	15
new word	shēngcí	生词	n	15**, 24
news	xīnwén	新闻	n	23
newspaper	bào	报	n	5**, 15
next year	míngnián	明年	n	20**, 29
nine	jiǔ	九	number	11
no, not	bù	不	adv	3
no, not	méi	没	adv	14

English meaning	Pinyin	Characters	Functions	Lesson
no, not	méi (you)	没(有)	adv	23
not bad	búcuò	不错	adj	25
note-book	běnzi	本子	n	11**, 13**
novel	xiǎoshuō	小说	n	26**
now, nowadays	xiànzài	现在	n	11
number	hào	号	n	10
number	hàomǎ	号码	n	23**
o'clock	diǎn	点	measure	17
Oceanaria	Dàyáng Zhōu	大洋洲	n-prop	7**
office worker	zhíyuán	职员	n	14**
often	cháng	常	adv	12
oh	à	啊	interj	13
old	jiù	旧	adj	16
on	shàngbiān	上边	n	22
once more	zài	再	adv	25
one	yī	一	number	10
opera	gējù	歌剧	n	26**
opposite	duìmiàn	对面	n	22
or	háishi	还是	conj	19
or	huòzhě	或者	conj	26
orange	júzi	桔子	n	19
orangeade, orange juice	júzishuǐ	桔子水	n	19
ought to	yīnggāi	应该	v-cog	26
outside	wàibiān	外边	n	22**
outside	wàibiān	外边	n	23
over	shàngbiān	上边	n	22
overcoat, topcoat	dàyī	大衣	n	16**
painting	huàr	画儿	n	26**
pair	shuāng	双	measure	28
Palanka	Pàlánkǎ	帕兰卡	prop	1*, 13*

English meaning	Pinyin	Characters	Functions	Lesson
paper	zhǐ	纸	n	5**, 13
park	gōngyuán	公园	n	28**
parlor	kètīng	客厅	n	22
particle, interrogative	ma	吗	particle	2
particle, interrogative	ne	呢	particle	2
particle, modal	le	了	particle	13
particle, modal	a	啊	particle	17
particle, modal	ba	吧	particle	21
particle, modal	ne	呢	particle	2
particle, structural	de	得	particle	25
particle, structural	de	的	particle	5
particular	yídìng	一定	adj	20
pastry	diǎnxin	点心	n	24
peasant	nóngmín	农民	n	24
pen	bǐ	笔	n	5**, 13
pencil	bǐ	笔	n	5**, 13
people	rénmín	人民	n	26
person	rén	人	n	6
photograph	zhàopiàn	照片	n	21**, 23
pictorial	huàbào	画报	n	11
picture	huàr	画儿	n	26**
picture	zhàopiàn	照片	n	21**, 23
piece	zhāng	张	measure	16
plane	fēijī	飞机	n	29
please	qǐng	请	v-act	8
poem	shīgē	诗歌	n	26**
point	diǎn	点	measure	17
polite	kèqi	客气	v-state	8
polite address to a lady	nǚshì	女士	n	9**
post office	yóujú	邮局	n	13**
present	lǐwù	礼物	n	21**

English meaning	Pinyin	Characters	Functions	Lesson
pretty	piàoliang	漂亮	adj	21
pretty good	búcuò	不错	adj	25
professor	jiàoshòu	教授	n	13**
progress	jìnbù	进步	n	29
proverb	chéngyǔ	成语	n	26
pupil	xiǎoxuéshēng	小学生	n	27**
quarter (or an hour)	kè	刻	measure	17
question	wèntí	问题	n	18
quick	kuài	快	adj	25
reading room	yuèlǎnshì	阅览室	n	15
real	zhēn	真	adj	21
reception	zhāodàihuì	招待会	n	27
red	hóng	红	adj	19
referee	cáipàn	裁判	n	28
refreshments	diǎnxin	点心	n	24
representative	dàibiǎo	代表	n	23
request	qǐng	请	v-act	8
research	yánjiū	研究	n	26
right	yòubiān	右边	n	22**
right away	jiù	就	adv	26
river	hé	河	n	25
road	lù	路	n	17
room	fángjiān	房间	n	22
ruler	chǐ	尺	n	5**
rural areas	nóngcūn	农村	n	24
sad	nánguò	难过	adj	29
scented tea	huāchá	花茶	n	19
schoolboy/girl	xiǎoxuéshēng	小学生	n	27**
schoolmate	tóngxué	同学	n	20
seat	zuòwèi	座位	n	16**
See you again	zàijiàn	再见	idiom	11

English meaning	Pinyin	Characters	Functions	Lesson
self	zì jǐ	自己	pron	30
serious	rènzhēn	认真	adj	24
set	tào	套	measure	22**
seven	qī	七	number	11
several	jǐ	几	number	15
Shanghai	Shànghǎi	上海	n-prop	7*
she	tā	她	pron	5
ship	chuán	船	n	29**
shirt	chènshān	衬衫	n	16
shoes	xié	鞋	n	28
shop	shāngdiàn	商店	n	13
should	yīnggāi	应该	aux v	26
side	pángbiān	旁边	n	22
sir	xiānsheng	先生	n	8**, 12
six	liù	六	number	11
skates	bīngxié	冰鞋	n	28
skating	huá bīng	滑冰	v-comb	28
skating boots	bīngxié	冰鞋	n	28
skiing	huá xuě	滑雪	v-comb	28**
skirt	qúnzi	裙子	n	16
slow	màn	慢	adj	25
small	xiǎo	小	adj	22
smoke	yān	烟	n	8
snack	diǎnxin	点心	n	24
so	suǒyǐ	所以	conj	29
some	xiē	些	measure	24
sometimes	yǒu shíhou	有时候	idiom	18
son	érzi	儿子	n	21**
song	gēr	歌儿	n	19
soup	tāng	汤	n	25
South America	Nán Měi Zhōu	南美洲	n-prop	7**

English meaning	Pinyin	Characters	Functions	Lesson
spare time	kòngr	空儿	n	20
spoken language	kǒuyǔ	口语	n	15
sports	yùndòng	运动	n	28**
spouse	àiren	爱人	n	14
squad	bān	班	n	15**, 20
stadium	tǐyùchǎng	体育场	n	28**
staff	zhíyuán	职员	n	14**
stamp	yóupiào	邮票	n	13**
state	guó	国	n	6
still	hái	还	adv	15
story (of a building)	céng	层	measure	10
storied building	lóu	楼	n	27
student	xuésheng	生	n	9
studious	nǔlì	努力	adj	29
study	shūfáng	书房	n	22
sugar	táng	糖	n	19**
suitcase	xiāngzi	箱子	n	28
summer	xiàtiān	夏天	n	29
Sunday	xīngqīrì	星期日	n	20
supper	wǎnfàn	晚饭	n	26**
surely	yídìng	一定	adv	20
surname	xìng	姓	n	9
surname (, one's) is...	xìng	姓	v-id	9
sweets	táng	糖	n	19**
swimming	yóuyǒng	游泳	v-comb, n	25
switchboard	zǒngjī	总机	n	23**
table	zhuōzi	桌子	n	22
table tennis	pīngpāngqiú	乒乓球	n	28**
tea	chá	茶	n	8
teacher	lǎoshī	老师	n	6
team	duì	队	n	28

English meaning	Pinyin	Characters	Functions	Lesson
telephone	diànhuà	电话	n	11**, 23
telephone call	diànhuà	电话	n	11**, 23
television	diànshì	电视	n	23
ten	shí	十	number	11
tennis	wǎngqiú	网球	n	28**
text	kèwén	课文	n	23
than	bǐ	比	prep	28
that	nà	那	pron	5
The Great Wall	Chángchéng	长城	n-prop	7*
The People's Daily	Rénmín Rì bào	人民日报	n-prop	23*
The Yangtze River	Cháng jiāng	长江	n-prop	7*
The Yellow River	Huáng Hé	黄河	n-prop	7*
the line is busy	zhàn xiàn	占线	idiom	23**
theatre	jùchǎng	剧场	n	16**
them	tāmen	他们	pron	3
them (for females)	tāmen	她们	pron	12
then	jiù	就	*conj	26
there	nàr	那儿	pron	10**
there	nàr	那儿	pron	15
there be	yǒu	有	v-poss.	14
therefore	suǒyǐ	所以	conj	29
they	tāmen	他们	pron	3
they (for females)	tāmen	她们	pron	12
thing	shì r	事儿	n	17
thing	dōngxi	东西	n	30
this	zhè	这	pron	4
this year	jīnnián	今年	n	20
three	sān	三	number	10
ticket	piào	票	n	16
tidy	zhěngqí	整齐	adj	25**
tight	jǐn	紧	adj	29

English meaning	Pinyin	Characters	Functions	Lesson
to	wèi	为	prep	27
to	gěi	给	co-v	14
to act as	dāng	当	v-id	26
to act as a referee	cáipàn	裁判	v-act	28
to answer	huídá	回答	v-act	24
to answer (the phone)	jiē (diànhuà)	接(电话)	v-act	23
to arrive	dào	到	v-act	27
to ask	wèn	问	v-act	9
to ask	ràng	让	v-act	19
to attend	bàn	办	v-act	28
to attend	cānjiā	参加	v-act	20
to attend or to teach (a class)	shàng(kè)	上课	v-act	17
to be	shì	是	v-id	4
to be at	zài	在	v-loc	10
to be at ease	fàng xīn	放心	idiom	29
to be beautiful	piàoliang	漂亮	v-state	21
to be big	dà	大	v-state	16
to be black	hēi	黑	v-state	16**
to be blue	lán	蓝	v-state	16**
to be busy	máng	忙	v-state	3
to be called	jiào	叫	v-id	9
to be called (or named) as	jiào	叫	v-id	9
to be conscientious	rènzhēn	认真	v-state	24
to be correct	duì	对	v-state	13
to be delighted	gāoxìng	高兴	v-state	21
to be difficult	nán	难	v-state	24
to be excited	gāoxìng	高兴	adj	21
to be few	shǎo	少	v-state	22
to be fond of	xǐhuan	喜欢	v-act	19
to be friendly	yǒuhǎo	友好	v-state	23
to be glad	gāoxìng	高兴	v-state	21

English meaning	Pinyin	Characters	Functions	Lesson
to be going to	yào	要	v-int	19
to be going to	yào	要	adv	29
to be good	hǎo	好	v-state	1
to be good-looking	hǎokàn	好看	v-state	21
to be happy	gāoxìng	高兴	adj	21
to be in	zài	在	v-loc	10
to be large	dà	大	v-state	16
to be like	xiàng	象	v-id	21
to be neat	gānjìng	干净	v-state	21**
to be new	xīn	新	v-state	15
to be old	jiù	旧	v-state	16
to be polite	kèqi	客气	v-state	8
to be pretty	piàoliang	漂亮	v-state	21
to be red	hóng	红	v-state	19
to be right	duì	对	v-state	13
to be short of	chà	差	v-state	17
to be small	xiǎo	小	v-state	22
to be tidy	zhěngqí	整齐	v-state	25**
to be well	hǎo	好	v-state	1
to be white	bái	白	v-state	16
to be willing	yuànyì	愿意	v-int	29
to be young	niánqīng	年轻	v-state	21
to beat	yíng	赢	v-act	28
to begin	kāishǐ	开始	v-act	27
to board	shàng	上	v-act	29
to borrow	jiè	借	v-act	15**
to buy	mǎi	买	v-act	13
to call (a taxi, etc.)	jiào	叫	v-act	29**
to call on	fǎngwèn	访问	v-act	23
to call on (a person)	zhǎo	找	v-act	16
to chat	tán	谈	v-act	20**, 26

English meaning	Pinyin	Characters	Functions	Lesson
to coach	fǔdǎo	辅导	v-act	20
to come	lái	来	v-act	13
to come in	jìn lái	进来	v-comb	26**
to come in	jìn	进	v-act	8
to come or go off work	xià bān	下班	idiom	17**
to come to a stop	tíng	停	v-act	25
to compare	bǐ	比	v-act	28
to compare	bǐjiào	比较	v-act	25**
to compete	sài	赛	v-act	28
to congratulate	zhùhè	祝贺	v-act	20
to cry	kū	哭	v-act	30
to dance	tiào wǔ	跳舞	v-comb	21
to deepen	jiāshēn	加深	v-act	26
to do	zuò	作	v-act	14
to do	bàn	办	v-act	28
to do physical training	duànliàn	锻炼	v-act	24
to draw	huà	画	v-act	26**
to drink	hē	喝	v-act	8
to drive (a car)	kāi (chē)	开(车)	v-act	23
to eat	chī	吃	v-act	18
to enter	jìn lái	进来	v-comb	26**
to enter	jìn	进	v-act	8
to exercise	yùndòng	运动	v-act	28**
to fall ill	bìng	病	v-state	27**
to fish with a hook and bait	diào	钓	v-act	25
to follow	gēn	跟	v-act	17
to forget	wàng	忘	v-act	29
to get along	guò	过	v-act	30
to get into	shàng	上	v-act	29
to get married	jié hūn	结婚	v-comb	20**
to get on	shàng	上	v-act	29

English meaning	Pinyin	Characters	Functions	Lesson
to get someone angry/annoyed	qì én	气人	idiom	28
to get up	qǐ chuáng	起床	idiom	18
to get up	qǐ	起	v-act	18
to give	sòng	送	v-act	21
to give	gěi	给	v-act	14
to give as a present	sòng	送	v-act	21
to go	qù	去	v-act	12
to go	zǒu	走	v-act	17
to go to bed	shuì jiào	睡觉	idiom	18
to go to work	shàng bān	上班	idiom	17**
to go to...	dào	到	v-act	27
to handle	bàn	办	v-act	28
to have	yǒu	有	v-poss.	14
to have a pleasant journey	yílùpíngān	一路平安	idiom	29
to have fun with	wánr	玩儿	v-act	23
to help	bāng	帮	v-act	22
to help	bāngzhu	帮助	v-act	22
to hire (a taxi, etc.)	jiào	叫	v-act	29**
to interpret, to translate	fānyi	翻译	v-act	26
to introduce	jièshao	介绍	v-act	13
to judge	cáipàn	裁判	v-act	28
to kick	tī	踢	v-act	28
to know	zhīdao	知道	v-cog	20
to know	rènshi	认识	v-cog	12
to know	liǎojiě	了解	v-cog	26
to know how to	huì	会	v-cog	26
to lack	chà	差	v-state	17
to laugh	xiào	笑	v-act	30
to learn	xué	学	v-act	9
to learn	xuéxí	学习	v-act	9
to leave	líkāi	离开	v-act	29

English meaning	Pinyin	Characters	Functions	Lesson
to lend	jiè	借	v-act	15**
to let	ràng	让	v-act	19
to like	xǐhuan	喜欢	v-act	19
to listen	tīng	听	v-act	19
to live	zhù	住	v-act	10
to live	guò	过	v-act	30
to look	kàn	看	v-act	7
to look for (a person)	zhǎo	找	v-act	16
to lose	shū	输	v-act	28
to make (a telephone call)	dǎ (diànhuà)	打 (电话)	v-act	23
to make progress	jìnbù	进步	v-act	29
to make use of	yòng	用	v-act	11
to meet	jiàn	见	v-act	29
to meet (a person)	jiē (rén)	接 (人)	v-act	23
to meet (to see) each other	jiànmiàn	见面	v-comb	29
to miss	xiǎng	想	v-act	14
to open	kāi	开	v-act	21
to paint	huà	画	v-act	26**
to part	fēnbié	分别	v-act	29
to pay a visit	cānguān	参观	v-act	23
to pay attention to	zhùyì	注意	v-act	29
to play	wánr	玩儿	v-act	23
to practice	liànxí	练习	v-act	24
to prepare	zhǔnbèi	准备	v-act	25
to progress	jìnbù	进步	v-act	29
to propose a toast	gānbēi	干杯	idiom	27
to put in order	zhěnglǐ	整理	v-act	22
to put on	chuān	穿	v-act	16
to reach	dào	到	v-act	27
to read	kàn	看	v-act	7

English meaning	Pinyin	Characters	Functions	Lesson
to read (aloud)	niàn	念	v-act	24
to recognize	rènshi	认识	v-cog	12
to reply	huídá	回答	v-act	24
to research	yánjiū	研究	v-act	26
to resemble	xiàng	象	v-id	21
to return	huán	还	v-act	11
to return	huí	回	v-act	17
to review	fùxí	复习	v-act	23
to rise	qǐ	起	v-act	18
to say	shuō	说	v-act	13
to see	jiàn	见	v-act	29
to see (someone) off	sòng (rén)	送(人)	v(-comb)-act	30
to see someone off	sòngxíng	送行	v-act	29**
to serve as	dāng	当	v-id	26
to set off	chūfā	出发	v-act	23
to set one's mind at rest	fàng xīn	放心	idiom	29
to sing	chàng	唱	v-act	19
to sit	zuò	坐	v-act	10
to skate	huá bīng	滑冰	v-comb	28
to ski	huá xuě	滑雪	v-comb	28**
to sleep	shuì jiào	睡觉	idiom	18
to smile	xiào	笑	v-act	30
to smoke	xī yān	吸烟	v-act	8
to speak	shuō	说	v-act	13
to stand	zhàn	站	v-act	29
to start	kāishǐ	开始	v-act	27
to start out	chūfā	出发	v-act	23
to stop	tíng	停	v-act	25
to straighten up	zhěnglǐ	整理	v-act	22
to study	xué	学	v-act	9

English meaning	Pinyin	Characters	Functions	Lesson
to study	xuéxí	学习	v-act	9
to study (a subject)	niàn	念	v-act	24
to swim	yóu yǒng	游泳	v-comb, n	25
to take a bath	xǐ zǎo	洗澡	v-act	22
to take a picture	zhào xiàng	照像	v-comb	29
to take a rest	xiūxi	休息	v-act	18
to take a seat	zuò	坐	v-act	10
to take off	qǐfēi	起飞	v-act	29
to take part in	cānjiā	参加	v-act	20
to talk	tán	谈	v-act	20**, 26
to taste	cháng	当	v-act	27
to teach	jiāo	教	v-act	15
to tell	gàosu	告诉	v-act	14
to thank	gǎnxiè	感谢	v-act	21
to thank	xièxie	谢谢	v-act	8
to think	xiǎng	想	v-act	14
to tour	lǚxíng	旅行	v-act	29**
to travel	lǚxíng	旅行	v-act	29**
to try	shì	试	v-act	27
to understand	dǒng	懂	v-cog	24
to understand	liǎojiě	了解	v-cog	26
to use	yòng	用	v-act	11
to visit	fǎngwèn	访问	v-act	23
to visit	cānguān	参观	v-act	23
to wait	děng	等	v-act	17
to walk	zǒu	走	v-act	17
to want	xiǎng	想	v-intention	14
to want	yào	要	v-act	19
to watch	kàn	看	v-act	7
to wear	chuān	穿	v-act	16
to weep	kū	哭	v	30

English meaning	Pinyin	Characters	Functions	Lesson
to welcome	huānyíng	欢迎	v-act	8
to win	yíng	赢	v-act	28
to wish	zhù	祝	v-act	21
to work	gōngzuò	工作	v	14
to work out	yùndòng	运动	v-act	28**
to write	xiě	写	v-act	14
today	jīntiān	今天	n	20
together	yìqǐ	一起	adv	17
toilet	cèsuǒ	厕所	n	10**
tomorrow	míngtiān	明天	n	23
too	yě	也	adv	2
too	tài	太	adv	16
top	shàngbiān	上边	n	22
train	huǒchē	火车	n	24
trainer	jiàoliàn	教练	n	25
translator	fānyì	翻译	n	26
trousers	kùzi	裤子	n	16**
true	zhēn	真	adj	21
two	liǎ	俩	measure	26
two	èr	二	number	10
two	liǎng	两	number	16
U.S.A.	Měiguó	美国	n-prop	6**
umbrella	yǔsǎn	雨伞	n	11**
umpire	cáipàn	裁判	n	28
(unit)	ge	个	measure	15
(unit)	jiàn	件	measure	16
(unit)	tiáo	条	measure	16
(unit)	zhī	枝	measure	19**
(unit)	bǎ	把	measure	22**
(unit, hat)	dǐng	顶	measure	28
(unit, person)	wèi	位	measure	25

English meaning	Pinyin	Characters	Functions	Lesson
(unit, vehicle)	liàng	辆	measure	21**
upper outer garment	shàngyī	上衣	n	16**
us	wǒmen	我们	pron	6
volleyball	páiqiú	排球	n	28**
vegetable	cài	菜	n	25**, 27
vehicle	qìchē	汽车	n	29**
very	fēicháng	非常	adv	21
very	hěn	很	adv	2
visa	qiānzhèng	签证	n	28
volume	běn	本	measure	15
waiter	fúwùyuán	服务员	n	19
waitress	fúwùyuán	服务员	n	19
Wang	Wáng	王	n-prop	8*, 15*
Wang Shuwen	Wáng Shūwén	王书文	n-prop	24*
want	yào	要	v-int	19
watch	biǎo	表	n	17**
water	shuǐ	水	n	19
way	lù	路	n	17
we	wǒmen	我们	pron	6
week	xīngqī	星期	n	20
well-known	yǒumíng	有名	adj	26
what	shénme	什么	pron	7
What's your (sur)name?	guì xìng	贵姓	idiom	9
where	nǎli	哪里	idiom	25
where	nǎr	哪儿	pron	10
which	nǎ	哪	pron	6
white	bái	白	adj	16
who	shéi	谁	pron	6
wife	tàitai	太太	n	8**, 21
will	yào	要	adv	29
window	chuānghu	窗户	n	22**

English meaning	Pinyin	Characters	Functions	Lesson
wine	jiǔ	酒	n	27
winter	dōngtiān	冬天	n	28
with	hé	和	conj	13
with	gēn	跟	co-v	17
word	cí	词	n	24
work	gōngzuò	工作	n	14
worker	gōngrén	工人	n	23
world	shìjiè	世界	n	7**
writer	zuòjiā	作家	n	26
year	nián	年	n	20
year (age)	suì	岁	measure	20
yesterday	zuótiān	昨天	n	28
you	nǐ	你	pron	1
you (pl.)	nǐmen	你们	pron	4
you (polite form of "nǐ")	nín	您	pron	8
young	niánqīng	年轻	adj	21
young lady	xiǎojie	小姐	n	9**, 19
younger brother	dìdi	弟弟	n	3
younger sister	mèimei	妹妹	n	14
zero	líng	零	number	10